PRAISE FOR SEVEN ARROWS

"*Seven Arrows* is an ideal book on Bible interpretation for the local church. It is clear, practical, and covers the essential bases of a well-rounded hermeneutic. Take your Bible teachers through this book and watch the Bible come alive in their classes. I am glad to commend its use for the building up of the Body of Christ."

Daniel L. Akin
President, Southeastern Baptist Theological Seminary

"Mathis and Rogers have come up with a creative, thoughtful, and practical way to teach church members how to study and apply the scriptures to their own lives. I especially appreciated the emphasis on biblical theology in interpretation and the role the church plays in application. The entire book is wise and useful and will help many to apply the Bible to their own lives."

Thomas R. Schreiner,
James Buchanan Harrison Professor of New Testament Interpretation, The Southern Baptist Theological Seminary

"Donny Mathis and Matt Rogers have provided an incredible resource for the church. In an era where many have neglected the simple commitment to reading the Bible every day, Donny and Matt do us a favor by pointing us back to this basic discipline and providing a simple path forward to making it a regular habit. You should read this book!"

Micah Fries

Pastor, Brainerd Baptist Church

"One of the most underrated and critical aspects of Christian growth and discipleship is the ability to 'self-feed' on the Word of God. As a pastor, equipping the congregation to do so might be my chief task apart from evangelism. I'm thankful Matt has written *Seven Arrows* and has given the church the process needed to feed itself."

Dean Inserra

Pastor, City Church Tallahassee

"Rogers and Mathis' *Seven Arrows* meets several significant needs in our churches today. It provides a discipleship resource for church members that centers on the Bible. It helps church members learn to read, understand, and apply God's word. Best of all, it is reproducible: any church member can share it with another believer, getting that believer started in a life-long process of discipleship. Highly recommended."

Bruce Ashford

Provost and Dean of the Faculty at Southeastern Baptist Theological Seminary

"The church's ability to read God's word has been crippled over the past several decades. That's why I'm so thankful for Rogers and Mathis' *Seven Arrows*. It uniquely helps new Christians and mature Christians read God's word personally and powerfully. I pray more churches would use this helpful tool to help their people become saturated with God's word."

Jedediah Coppenger
Lead Pastor, Redemption City Church, Nashville, TN

"Making disciples in Boston is not light work, but God's word is sufficient for the task. As we equip disciple-makers to make more disciple-makers, the Seven Arrows of Bible Reading have proved to be a simple and reproducible tool for taking people deeper into the stream of God's transforming grace."

Tanner Turley
Lead Pastor, Redemption Hill Church, Boston, MA

"I love the extremely simple but powerful framework that my friends have developed in this book. *Seven Arrows* is going to equip you to better understand, connect, and apply the Bible. This work is a must read for all disciple-makers!"

Rob Wilton
Lead Pastor, Vintage Church, New Orleans, LA

"Matt Rogers and Donny Mathis have created an excellent guide for studying Scripture in the context of community. This resource will help local churches in their effort to increase Bible literacy while at the same time create environments for people to be in relationship with one another. These men are both scholars and authors, but at their heart they are pastors who care for their people. This book is an outgrowth of their work in the local church."

Aaron Coe

Executive Director of Expansion: Passion Network

"Before he ascended to the throne, Jesus gave clear final instructions to his followers: make disciples. But, we often have a hard time figuring out how to do that practically. That's why I love *Seven Arrows*. It gives a simple explanation for how to read the Bible, understand it and apply it to our lives. Any discipleship group would find this book invaluable."

Jon Akin

Pastor, Fairview Church

"*Seven Arrows* is not a commentary, but it will help readers understand the Bible better. It's not a homiletics text but it will help readers teach the Bible more clearly. It is for pastors and lay people alike and offers a helpful method for reading and understanding the Bible without spoon-feeding a reader's interpretation. I love books like this because they help me learn *how* to think instead of telling me *what* to read. Matt Rogers and Donny Mathis have given Christians a real gift with this book."

Barnabas Piper
Author and podcaster

SEVEN ARROWS

Aiming Bible Readers in the Right Direction

Matt Rogers and Donny Mathis

Seven Arrows:
Aiming Bible Readers in the Right Direction

© 2017 by Matt Rogers and Donny Mathis

Rainer Publishing
Spring Hill, TN
www.RainerPublishing.com

ISBN 978-0-9978861-8-4

Printed in the United States of America.

For the Church.

ACKNOWLEDGEMENTS

Books are tools to serve the church. The time, effort, and energy it takes to write a useful book is foolish unless the project aids the church in fulfilling its God-ordained purpose. The best books, it seems, are written to aid the church in solving a problem—either in thinking or in living. We hope this book does both.

The Church at Cherrydale in Greenville, South Carolina has provided a fertile context for developing a tool that would help people read, understand, and apply the Bible to their lives. It has also given us an army of would-be disciple-makers who long to be faithful to the command of Jesus to make disciples until he returns. We know that this task necessitates our people grow to feed themselves a steady diet of the meat of God's word.

I (Donny) am very thankful to God for the opportunity to serve his church by teaching his word both at North Greenville University and at The Church at Cherrydale. I pray that he takes the fruit of that labor and helps those who read this book. As I write these words of thanks, I struggle to put into words the ways that my wife, Amber, has supported, encouraged, exhorted, and loved me over these ten years. During the writing of this book, we have faced some difficult trials, but she sacrificed time and sleep to help see this book through to its conclusion. She is simply the best! To my son, when you are able to read, I pray that this book would serve to increase the love you already have for the "Bibey" and that you would serve King Jesus with all that you are. To my parents, thank you for instilling in me a love and reverence for the Bible and modeling every day what it looks like to love and serve Jesus well. To Matt, I want to thank you for your graciousness to include me in writing this book and your patience with me through the process of completing it. Finally, I want to thank Dr. Robert H. Stein for teaching me how to think carefully about how to interpret the Bible and how to be a truly Christian scholar.

I (Matt) have the joy of learning to teach the Bible as a father, disciple-maker, and pastor of the local church. Each of these circles are worthy of thanks. I am first and foremost a pastor of my home and owe my "little-church" a debt of gratitude for their gracious love, support, and trust. Sarah consistently makes me feel far smarter than I actually am, and her constant encouragement and unending love provides the motivation to write a book such as this. My kids, Corrie, Avery, Hudson, and Willa, are at the heart of why I wrote this book—I want them to love Jesus and his word for the rest of their lives. Second, I am shaped by the investment that I have attempted to make in others' lives. It is one thing to preach a rousing sermon and quite another to disciple a single individual as he seeks to understand and apply the Bible to his life. I have been shaped as much by those I have discipled as I hope they have been shaped by me. Finally, as a pastor of a local church I know that God will transform our people by his word more than anything else. I pray that the culture of our church is such that people are led to hunger for the word and be transformed as a result. Relationships with men like Donny have refined and encouraged my pursuit of Christ through his word.

We pray that God would multiply our meager efforts in the pages ahead to strengthen and build his church by the power of his wondrous word.

Matt and Donny

CONTENTS

PREFACE

How'd he do that? The expression was almost audible. I (Matt) remember listening to a preacher teach a familiar passage on the radio while sitting in my green Ford Ranger pickup in the parking lot at Furman University. I had read the text numerous times since my conversion due to my seemingly insatiable hunger for God's word. Yet, hearing this skilled pastor proclaim the Scriptures faithfully brought out a depth of meaning and beauty I didn't see when reading the Bible alone.

Honestly, I was stunned and frustrated. Why hadn't I seen that? What was he doing that allowed him to notice nuances and complexities of the Scripture that I did not? Would it require a seminary degree, perhaps even a PhD, to read the Bible, understand its meaning, and apply it to my life?

Now, as a pastor of a local church who writes and preaches regularly, I hear people ask me that question. They share how the word has challenged, convicted, and spurred them on to spiritual maturity. And for that I am thankful.

I am also scared. I am afraid that I may subtly create a chasm between the average member of the church that I serve and me. I am frightened that they may depend on me for too much. I am scared that this may produce passivity in them, thinking that somehow I am doing something they can never do for themselves. And, I am convicted that my God-given role is to equip God's saints for the work of the ministry which means I have a responsibility to teach them to feast on God's word for themselves (Eph 4:11–16).

Everyone who attends the local church I pastor will not stand before large groups of people and teach the Scriptures regularly. Some will. Most will not. What they will do is awaken every day with a treasure sitting on a shelf in their house—God's revealed word. *What they do with their Bible will shape the trajectory of their lives.*

This reality became clear to me during the first year after planting a church in Greenville, South Carolina in 2010. God saved a young man in our congregation, and he was filled with questions. Like most new Christians, he wanted to know God deeply and asked me to help him. We met over breakfast once a week and talked about life and faith. Each question led to another series of questions and a quest deeper into God's word.

His passion was great for the 90 minutes or so we were together each week. But what was he doing for the rest of the week? I knew that he was reading his Bible, but I also knew that he did not have a plan. He did not know where to start, what to read, or what to do while he was reading. This led to mounting confusion and doubt on his part.

I had to develop a plan to help him read his Bible effectively. But this could not be just any plan. It could not be overly academic. My friend, while filled with spiritual vitality, was not a theology student. He'd never read the Bible before on his own, much less heard the word "hermeneutics." If I gave him a thick book of theological "do's and don'ts," I knew that it would only heighten his insecurities with God's word.

I also did not want to give him some other author's reflections on the Bible. Don't get me wrong. Devotional guides are necessary and helpful tools for the church, but my friend needed to start with the Bible rather than training himself to depend on someone else to do the work for him. If I handed him another devotional guide I would be doing the same thing that I wanted to avoid in my preaching—I would teach him to depend on a middleman to help him read the Bible.

Finally, I wanted to avoid giving my friend something overly simplistic. I knew there were Bible reading methods available, but I could not find one that would give them a map for reading that could be used with any passage of Scripture. Sure, they could note things they observed about a Bible passage and how that passage affected their lives, but I wanted him to dig deeper for himself—to not simply scratch the surface but to mine the gem that is God's word. I also wanted my friend and those who would come after him to have an ordered plan so they would not just be asking random questions about the Bible but asking good questions and asking them in the right order. This tool would allow him to study the Bible on his own for the rest of his life.

I doodled on a dinner napkin the questions I ask when reading a passage of Scripture, and I used directional arrows to illustrate my meaning. Little forethought went into the doodle other than years of personal Bible reading and reflection.

I started with Arrow 1–a circular arrow that wraps around itself making a dot. Arrow 1 asks, *What does this passage say?*

What does this passage say?

First, I wanted him to summarize the passage in a simple sentence or two, restating the main point of the text in his own words. Whether a parable, historical narrative, or wisdom passage, God sustained every text with a clear purpose. A basic understanding of what the text says is essential before moving forward.

From there, Arrow 2 was a backward pointing arrow and asked, *What did this passage mean to its original audience?*

What does this passage mean to its original audience?

Long before we can ever discern the implications of a passage for our lives, we must consider what the text meant to its first hearers.

Arrow 3 pointed up and asked the reader to consider, *What does this passage tell us about God?*

What does this passage tell us about God?

The Trinitarian God of the Bible is the main character of every passage. His person and work are always on display. In some places, God the Father is center stage, at other times, the person of Jesus is, and elsewhere the work of the Holy Spirit is. If the reader sees God clearly, answering the questions prompted by Arrows 4–7 will be much easier.

What does this passage tell us about man? is the question posed by Arrow 4.

What does this passage tell us about man?

Here the reader must grapple with how text demonstrates the fallen, sinful condition of people apart from God or the graciously, redeemed picture of life for those in Christ.

From there, the reader is ready to answer the question that often gets the most attention and is raised in Arrow 5. *What does this passage demand of me?*

What does this passage demand of me?

Modern readers are quick to create personalized application of biblical texts, in which they rip the passage from its biblical context and apply it in an unclear, unhelpful, or incorrect way; however, with the context of Arrows 1–4 in place, the reader is now positioned to make personal application from the text properly.

Arrow 6 forces a corporate application of the biblical text. The Christian faith—and by implication, the Bible—is understood within the community of the church and in mission to the world. Growth in Christ-likeness through application of the word requires the community of the local church. Love, trust, encouragement, etc. are difficult to practice in isolation. As a result, Arrow 6 asks the reader to consider, *How does this passage change the way I relate to people?*

How does this passage change
the way I relate to people?

Finally, Arrow 7 ends with prayer. Not just any prayer, but prayer rooted in the Scriptures and derived from the passage under consideration. *What does this text prompt me to pray?*

What does this text
prompt me to pray?

Asking this question is a proper way to end time spent in God's word and allows for prayers that are informed, sustained, and amplified by a right understanding of God as seen in the Bible.

That's it. I formulated a simple process that would aid my brother in reading the Bible for himself, understanding the intended meaning, and applying that meaning to his life.

I never intended these simple doodles to go beyond that breakfast table. But they have. Disciples of Jesus are hungry for simple, practical tools to aid them in knowing God and making him known. I have watched disciple-makers in our church use these Arrows to help a new believer grow in faith and understanding. I have watched teenagers read the Bible for themselves and unearth deep and profound truths of God's word. I have watched missionaries in other countries translate and use these Arrows to aid in mission to unreached parts of the world for the first time. I have seen other churches take these Arrows and use them to shape a disciple-making culture in their church, proving that normal church members can be faithful in the tasks of studying the Bible and disciple-making.

This brings me great joy as a pastor.

I still knew there were weaknesses in the Arrows. They provided a clear path, but the path needed light along the way. The Arrows force the reader to ask the right questions, but the answers may still be difficult to see. For example, how does a reader discern what the text meant to its original readers (Arrow 2)? Or, what if the passage seems to say something about God that makes little sense (Arrow 3)?

This book is an effort to illuminate the path down which the Arrows point.

The answers to these questions often prompt lengthy, academic resources that are seemingly inaccessible to the modern Bible reader. That doesn't have to be the case though. I have watched our congregation, The Church at Cherrydale in Greenville, South Carolina, grow under the teaching of men like Dr. Donny Mathis. We have worked diligently to take the simple Arrows I developed and teach our congregation to be effective Bible-readers.

For that reason, I asked Donny to help me turn this teaching into a simple book designed to shed increased light on the Arrows and clarify how a reader should go about answering those questions properly. This task serves as the basis of Donny's training and vocation. As a graduate of The Southern Baptist Theological Seminary with a PhD in New Testament and a professor of Greek, hermeneutics, and New Testament among other things, he is trained to speak to this issue well; however, he is far from an ivory tower theologian. His greatest strength is that he is a faithful member of our local church where he also serves as a lay elder. From this position, he provides practical tools that can aid anyone seeking to read and understand the Bible better and not simply those seeking a theological degree.

Our hope in writing this book is that we will fulfill our task of equipping the church (and not just The Church at

Cherrydale) for the work of the ministry (Eph 4:11–16). This will mean that church members can be weaned off of a reliance upon a pastor to do for them what they should do for themselves. It also means that disciples of Jesus who long to be faithful to the Great Commission will have a reproducible tool for disciple-making whether they read the Bible with a co-worker over lunch, discuss it with a friend while working out at the local gym, or disciple their kids during family devotions. Finally, it means that pastors of a local church can have a tool to foster a Bible-reading and obeying culture in their church body. Not only can the church know how the pastor puts together clear sermons, but they can be equipped to read and apply the Bible for themselves every day of the week.

The first edition of this book, published in 2015, has been used to disciple and train Bible readers around the world, and we are thrilled to now offer a revised edition through Rainer Publishing. We pray that the fruit of our labor will produce an army of God's people who will be unleashed on a disciple-making mission, which will lead to awestruck, life-encompassing worship as they are transformed by God's word.

INTRODUCTION:
WHY WRITE A BOOK
ABOUT THE BOOK?

God transforms his people by his word.

This claim separates this book from a guide to understanding organic chemistry or Newtonian physics. Our mission, in contrast, is not to gain knowledge about the Bible but to be transformed by it.

God has promised to transform his people. Paul tells the church in Rome that "those whom he foreknew he also predestined to be conformed to the image of his Son, in order that he might be the firstborn among many brothers. And those whom he predestined he also called, and those whom he called he also justified, and those whom he justified he also glorified" (Rom 8:29–30). We need not doubt what God is doing in the lives of his people–he is at work to conform them to the image of his Son.

When God spoke all of creation into existence, he showed that his words have power. That same power is at work as God continues to speak through his inspired word to recreate his people into glorious reflections of Jesus. As the writer of Hebrews explains, this word is "living and active, sharper than any two-edged sword, piercing to the division of soul and of spirit, of joints and of marrow, and discerning the thoughts and intentions of the heart" (Heb 4:12). The living word can bring transformation to all people since "no creature is hidden from his sight" (Heb 4:13). God still speaks and transforms today through his word.

Overstating the importance of the word of God in the life of the Christian is impossible. A direct correlation exists between a person's intake of the Scripture and his conformity to the image of Christ. As Kevin DeYoung writes, "You and I simply will not mature as quickly, minister as effectively, or live as gloriously without immersing ourselves in the Scriptures."[1] There are no shortcuts, nor alternative methods for transformation; therefore, God's people must learn to feast on his word.

Seven Arrows is intended to aid God's people in doing just that—feasting on the word of God. For this to happen, we must have a common understanding of what we believe about the Bible. A method for reading the Bible is impotent without a robust theological foundation. The purpose of this book is not to construct an apologetic for the doctrine of Scripture. Other books tackle that lofty goal.[2]

Nevertheless, each Arrow is predicated on certain core beliefs about the Bible. Think of these core beliefs as the first dot you make when you draw each Arrow. You can't draw an arrow without making a dot. Whatever the direction, each Arrow begins with an initial point. In the same way, one's core beliefs about the Bible form the point from which any method of Bible reading originates. What a person believes about the Bible will inform how the study of the Bible is approached. The following claims about God's word form the dot from which each of the *Seven Arrows* is drawn.

THE BIBLE IS A REVEALED WORD

God speaks. This claim should not be taken lightly. The silence of the universe was broken by the word of God (Gen 1–2). God's powerful word created all things and by it all things are held together (Heb 1:3). The Psalmist revels in this thought as he declares, "By the word of the Lord the heavens were made, and by the breath of his mouth all their hosts" (Ps 33:6). The voice of God bellows through his good creation and echoes back the glorious wonder of his majesty.

God did not speak in creation alone, but he provided a specific revelation of himself and his purposes in Holy Scripture. There, God's nature, character, and work are on full display with clarity that cannot be seen in creation alone. The Bible is the word of God revealed by God to display God. It does not merely contain some of God's words but is, in its entirety, the word of God. The biblical refrain "thus says the Lord" serves as the Bible's overarching truth claim. What the Bible says, God says.

God did not have to speak. He did not have to reveal himself. And He did not have to reveal himself in a way that his created beings could understand. Think for a moment about the stunning magnitude of this claim: the glorious God of the universe chose to reveal himself to his people by his word. Our frail, feeble, and fallen minds would be entirely incapable of knowing God had he not revealed himself to us.

THE BIBLE IS A GRACIOUS WORD

For this reason, the word of God is a gift of grace. It was a humbling act for the God of the universe to stoop to human words to reveal himself—much less to reveal himself to sin-drenched humans! Nothing about mankind deserves to hear from God. In fact, our fallenness means that we doubt, distort, and despise the voice of God even when he speaks, but God uses his word as the Spirit reveals its truth to transform people into Christians. As a result, those whose hearts have been awakened to the beauty of the gospel long for the word of God. A hunger for the word results from a heart stunned by hearing and responding to God at all. The Bible is a gift.

The authors of the Bible speak about God's word in this way. They write love poems to the Bible (Ps 19; 119) and call it a treasure. "I love them [your words] exceedingly" is the song of a worshiper of God. The prophet Jeremiah says, "Your words were found, and I ate them, and your words became to me a joy and a delight for my heart, for I am called by your name, O LORD, God of hosts" (Jer 15:16). No one speaks of obligations this way. You speak of gifts this way. The word of God is a gift from a gracious God.

THE BIBLE IS A CLEAR WORD

God gave the grace gift of the Scriptures to be understood. God is not a God of confusion, and his word is not meant to confound. There is no prerequisite course of spiritual maturity required to read the Bible. You don't have to pastor a local church or hold a seminary degree. God's word is a clear record of his person, work, and mission in the world that can be understood by all Christians.

Those who are reading the Bible for the first time may doubt this claim. The cultural distance between the Bible and modern readers makes reading the Bible seem intimidating. The words are big, the names and places are unrecognizable, and many of the stories are. . . well. . . strange!

Yet, we need not lose heart. God wants to be known. He did not reveal himself to make us more confused about who he is. He is not out to trick us or to bore us with mindless complexity. He gave us his word as an act of love so all people might worship him rightly. The Bible can make the simple mind wise (Ps 19:7; 119:130).

The Bible is not a simple book. Since it records the work of God throughout all human history, we should not be surprised to find that the Bible is complex. But the Bible can be both complex *and* clear. While feeble humans can never understand God fully, we can know him rightly.

A right understanding of God's word will require work. Even Peter claimed that Paul's words were challenging for him to understand, demanding discipline to read the Bible correctly (2 Pet 3:16). The purpose of *Seven Arrows* is to train all Christians, regardless of age, education, or maturity to apply a proper strategy to the study of God's word and understand its intended meaning to live out the mission that God has called them to complete.

THE BIBLE IS A TRUE WORD

A revealed, gracious, clear word will always be a true word. God, by his nature, cannot lie. So, when he speaks, he can be trusted to speak truthfully (2 Tim 3:16). The Bible commends its truthfulness consistently (Ps 119:42; Prov 30:5). Jesus himself treated the Scriptures as the word of God and exhorted his followers to trust it without reservation. The promised Holy Spirit was provided to transform and strengthen all subsequent disciples by the means of the word and not some alternative path.

Jesus prays that the Father would "sanctify them in the truth. . . your word is truth" (Jn 17:17). The Father's work of sanctification through the word transforms and empowers the church because "When you received the word of God, which you heard from us, you accepted it not as the word of men but as what it really is, the word of God, which is at work in you believers" (1 Thess 2:13).

That human authors recorded the word of God does not undermine this claim that the Bible is true. These authors, carried along by God's Spirit, used their unique personalities and contexts to trace the redemptive plan of God (2 Pet 1:21). The theological term for this truth claim is "inerrancy," meaning that the Bible, in its original form, is without error and true in all it affirms to the degree of precision intended by the author. For this reason, the Bible is the standard of truth—not modern science or human reason.

THE BIBLE IS A UNITED WORD

In order for the Bible to be clear, it must tell a unified story of God's work in the world. The Bible is composed of 66 books, written by dozens of authors, on three continents, over thousands of years. Yet, the Bible tells one story which crescendos in the person and work of Jesus Christ. On the road to Emmaus, Jesus encourages the travelers by showing them how the entire word of God pointed to him.

> *Then he said to them, 'These are my words that*
> *I spoke to you while I was still with you, that*
> *everything written about me in the Law of Moses*
> *and the Prophets and the Psalms must be fulfilled.'*
> *Then he opened their minds to understand the*
> *Scriptures, and said to them, 'Thus it is what is*
> *written, that the Christ should suffer and on the*
> *third day rise from the dead' (Luke 24:44–46).*

This is not some mystical story of a make-believe world, but rather the story of the mission of God from the creation of the world to his ultimate work to undo the effects of Satan, sin, and death. This unified story is the story of the Bible (1 Cor 15:3–4; Acts 3:18, 21, 24; 17:2, 3; 26:22, 23; 1 Pet 1:11). For many, understanding the Bible as one, united story of God's redemptive mission is a significant "light bulb" moment in their spiritual journey. Effort has been made throughout the *Seven Arrows* to demonstrate the united nature of the word of God and the way such an understanding helps the reader better understand God's intent.

THE BIBLE IS A SUFFICIENT WORD

God has given us all we need for life and godliness in his word (2 Pet 1:3). We need not look elsewhere for guidance, but rather deeper into the word we already have. This claim does not mean that the Bible answers every question such as who to marry, where to go to college, or which house you should buy. Rather, it provides sufficient insight into every question that is essential for knowing God and living the life we were designed to live. It is, as Paul writes "able to make you wise for salvation through faith in Christ Jesus" (2 Tim 3:15). This faith "comes from hearing, and hearing from the word of God" (Rom 10:17).

Those who understand this claim long to know the word of God (Ps 119:18, 19, 27, 29, 33, 34, 35, 64, 66, 73, 124, 125, 135, 169). No one, when standing before God on the last day, will blame God for withholding information from him. We all have more than enough in the Bible to be "equipped for every good work" (2 Tim 3:16–17). We must all be careful not to distort God's precious word by adding to it or taking away from it (Deut 4:2; 12:32; Prov 30:5–6; Rev 22:18–19). The grave consequences threatened for those who distort God's word reveal the care that God has taken to say exactly what he wanted to say.

THE BIBLE IS A NECESSARY WORD

The magnitude of the claims we have made about the Bible reveals how necessary the word of God is in the life of all Christians and in the church. We need God to reveal himself and his ways to us lest we incessantly grope around in the darkness. Our depraved hearts are incapable of figuring life out on our own.

Jesus told his first disciples that following him is predicated on learning to "observe all that I [Jesus] have commanded you" (Matt 28:20). This task is impossible without the word of God. The word of God is the primary tool God uses to demonstrate his glory and protect from sin, recording his will perfectly, protecting the church, and training believers in righteousness. We should seek to hide God's word in our hearts so that we might not sin against him (Ps 119:11). The word of God becomes like our daily nourishment, essential to life, health, and well-being (Matt 4:4).

The greatest danger in our day would be a famine of the word of God (Amos 8:11). Yet, hearing the Bible alone will not be enough. We must, as James exhorts us, "Be doers of the word and not hearers only, deceiving ourselves" (Jam 1:22).

CONCLUSION

This is the word of God: revealed, gracious, clear, true, united, sufficient, and necessary. For these reasons, God's word has the power to transform lives.

These truths about God's word serve as the dot that drives each Arrow in this plan. They are essential for reading the Bible correctly.

Now the fun begins.

We embark on the quest to know God by his word. Like the people of Berea in Acts 17, we must dig through the pages of our Bibles diligently to discern the heart and mind of God (Acts 17:11). In so doing, our lives will be transformed and our churches filled with proper worship. As the word of Christ dwells in us richly, it will increasingly transform us all into radiant reflections of the King of Glory (Col 3:16).

ARROW 1:
WHAT DOES
THIS PASSAGE SAY?

Why do we get sucked into certain stories? Why do we want to read or watch them repeatedly? Great stories yank us into a new world, drop us into the troubled lives of the characters, and entice to engage with them on an emotional level. We ache through the trials that a couple endures to find true love. We beat our chests (metaphorically, of course) over the triumph of our hero in battle. We long to have the strength to sacrifice for the good of those around us. These stories never become stale. The characters never bore us. Rather, every encounter with them highlights significant, new facets to the story even when we think that we know the plot by heart. Engaging with God by reading the Bible demands the same kind of attentiveness and enthusiasm that we invest in our favorite stories and characters.

I know some people struggle to engage with stories, especially ones they read, but they still desire to know

God deeply. They possess zeal and not skill. In fact, the idea of "connecting" with the Bible might sound strange to them; however, my guess is that they are drawn into stories every day on the television, in a movie, or with their favorite sports team. The ability to understand these stories had to be developed as well. Why should the Bible be any different?

In the end, avid and frustrated readers can both get bogged down in their attempts to study the Bible. The goal of Arrow 1 is to encourage all readers to examine and to engage the Bible with a clear goal in mind. In fact, not having a clear goal when they sit down to read the Bible might be *the* source of the frustration. Our first goal should be to determine what the passage says.

To answer the question posed by Arrow 1, we must discern the single point that the author is making in the paragraph or individual story we are examining. We accomplish this goal by observation. First, we must consider how the biblical authors communicate by determining whether the author is using literal language, like in a math book, or figurative language, like in a love song. Once we know the kind of language the author is using, we will develop basic observational techniques that will assist us in figuring out what the passage says and start us on the path to understanding the Bible and applying it accurately.

As you begin this journey of using the arrows and

pointing them in the right direction, you might be intimidated because the Bible does not feel or look like the typical book you would pick up to read. It might be bigger than any book you have ever read. And, it is *The Holy Bible*, for cryin' out loud! So, it must be even harder to understand than it looks. Then, you look at the Table of Contents, and it has a bunch of strange names, which probably means that strange people writing with strange words authored these books.

Stop psyching yourself out!

The problem is not that the Bible cannot be understood. The problem is that you are likely just not familiar enough with the Bible. Your pastor is not necessarily a genius. He has just developed skills for reading the Bible well. This book will give you some understanding of the entire Bible (both story and style). But, the key is to learn to hit the target by taking the aiming techniques we will provide and using them to help you understand a Bible passage's meaning. Any skill worth having takes work. The skill of understanding the Bible is no different. We practice until we are skillful because we think the skill is important. We learn to drive a car because the ability to get around on our own without walking or pedaling is important to us. We learn to talk because grunting and pointing is frustrating. Understanding the Bible is more important than any of these. So, practice these techniques!

So, take a deep breath. You can do this!

WRITING STYLE

The different styles and authors can make understanding the Bible a challenge at times. Examining how biblical writers present their material begins with figuring out what literary genre (or styles of writing) they have employed. Is the author recounting a story? Is the passage a song? Is it a prophecy? Once we answer this question, we can know whether the author will use literal language in the text or figurative, emotion-sparking language to teach his readers.[3]

The largest class of literature in the Bible is historical narrative. The narrative provides the skeletal structure for the story of God's work to establish and redeem his creation. The genres in the rest of the biblical writings are the muscles, organs, and tendons that attach to the skeleton. Some of these genres include prophecy, poetry, proverbs, parables, songs, idioms, exaggeration, laws, covenants, sermons, and letters. When these are attached to the skeleton, they work together to display not only what God does but also who he is.

These genres can be interwoven or one particular writing style can dominate and entire section or book in the Bible. You might find a prophetic word that appears within the flow of a historical narrative (1 Kings 17:1; 21:17-29), but prophecy can also stand alone as a literary genre that dominates entire books such as Isaiah, Jeremiah, Ezekiel, and the Minor Prophets. As the biblical writers recount the preaching of Jesus and others prophets, they often will relate how they used proverbs, parables (both verbal and acted lessons), idioms, exaggeration, and puns as tools in their teaching. Authors can even employ songs as a break in the middle of the story to recount the praise of the people for the great things that God has done (See Exod 14-15). In addition, proverbs and songs stand as the dominant genre in whole books, such as Job, Proverbs, Ecclesiastes, Psalms, Song of Solomon, and Lamentations.

Covenants (or treaties) and laws often appear within the narrative of the Old Testament. Some books, like Leviticus, use these genres almost exclusively. Be careful not to underestimate the importance of the covenants that God establishes with his people, particularly the Abrahamic Covenant (Gen 12, 15, 17). This relationship that God established and took the responsibility to fulfill provides the rationale for God's activity to bless, curse, and restore his people and comes to the forefront both in the historical narratives and the preaching of the prophets.

In the New Testament, some authors wrote letters because they could not come to the city at that time. In these letters, they would encourage the churches both to persevere in the faith and correct their thinking about the good news concerning the death and resurrection of Jesus the Messiah. They would build upon this theological foundation by explaining how these truths should change their actions in everyday situations. And, God still uses these books to correct our thinking about himself, what he has done, and then how to apply those truths in our lives.

The biblical authors use two kinds of language when they write—literal and figurative.[4] When authors employ *literal language*, the main goal is to convey information in a straightforward fashion with no symbolic meaning. As a result, what the author intends to teach is equal to the meaning of the actual words he uses. *Figurative language*, however, should alert us to the fact that the author intended to present a message that is not equal to the literal meaning of the words that he used. Remember that the biblical authors wanted to communicate a literal message, but this goal does not demand that they always use words literally.

You and I communicate with other people daily and use both of these types of language without even thinking. Have you ever used exaggeration to make a point to your child, spouse, or co-workers? (*She almost gave me a heart attack!*) Have you ever given someone directions? (*Drive 1.2 miles, and turn left onto Main Street.*) In both instances you had a literal meaning you wanted to convey, though only one example used literal language. Why should we expect the biblical writers to avoid using every literary tool at their disposal to convey the content of the biblical story? Biblical authors used a variety of genres to engage our minds and emotions so we can connect with the passage better and be changed by it.

This short discussion of genre and language leads to the conclusion that the literary context controls what individual words and paragraphs mean. *Context is king.* Words have no specific meaning until you use them in a sentence. For instance, when you pick up a dictionary, you could close your eyes, open it up, place your finger on the page, and find a word that has multiple meanings. (I don't recommend this process for picking a passage to study in the Bible). When you use the term in a sentence, most of the options will not make sense, and you will know the specific meaning of the word for that sentence. (*He mowed the yard. He gained a yard on that play.* The meaning of "yard" is clear because of the context of the sentence.)

This best and most fruitful reading of the Bible will be one in which we are constantly examining the individual passage to determine how it functions within the larger goals that the author has stated in the book. This task might seem daunting, but several tools will aid you in this process. When studying a particular book, begin by reading the whole book with the goal of knowing the overall picture of what happens and what is being described in the book. This initial reading will prepare you for the close observations you will be making as you employ the tools below.

TOOLS OF THE TRADE

In this section, we will provide some tools to use in your observation of the biblical text. These tools are not unique to us, and multiple authors have explained these methods for studying the Bible. [5] We hope that their implementation within the framework of *Seven Arrows* will help you have a better understanding of what the biblical authors intended to teach in a passage and will also help you understand new points of application. The list is not exhaustive, but we believe it is complete. These tools will help you understand what the passage says in most any genre:

- Repetition of Words and Themes
- Comparisons
- Figures of Speech
- Action
- Phrases and Clauses
- Conversations
- Lists
- Tone

Using these tools as you examine the text will help you compose a clear picture of the point that the author was making. If you are not a grammarian (or don't know what that is), don't panic. We will now discuss these tools at length.

Repetition of Words and Themes

This tool seems simplistic. It is so simple that we use it every day in conversations without even thinking. When my wife needs me to run an errand, she will use various modes of communication to repeat that she needs me to do something so that I will not forget. When I teach a class, I repeat main ideas numerous times so my students will remember the information for a question on a test or the due date for an assignment. So, common sense tells us that if something is repeated, it is important.

If it is such common sense, why do people who read the Bible forget to consider repetition in a passage? Think about Paul's letters as an example. He wrote to churches that had turmoil over all kinds of theological and ethical questions. In fact, humanly speaking, Paul would have written little if not for the headaches that the churches gave him. One thing that stands out when you read his work is Paul repeats himself to hammer the main points into his readers. Other biblical authors will do the same thing. Therefore, paying attention to how authors repeat themselves (even in using nouns and verbs from the same family, like "faith" and "believe") or use the same word differently within a passage will give us some insight into what is important and what they are communicating in a given passage.

Comparisons

A simple way to bring clarity into a conversation about a confusing concept is to draw a comparison or contrast that uses words or ideas the person you are trying to communicate with will understand immediately. Think about conversations you have had today. I can almost guarantee you have made a comparison or drawn a contrast to explain what you said (*ride like the wind* or *hot as fire*). Sometimes we use the words "like" or "as" to make a comparison and the words "but" or "however" to establish a contrasting idea. The biblical authors often used comparisons and contrasts to make difficult theological concepts accessible in everyday language. So, pay attention to the comparisons and contrasts because they can provide clues that help us interpret the meaning in a passage.

Figures of Speech

A figure of speech is a close cousin to a comparison. An author uses a figure of speech to create an indirect comparison in which the meaning of the words differs from, or even contradicts, their regular, literal usage. Readers can understand the meaning of these figures because they are used often to convey an emphatic message. For instance, when someone says that she has a "splitting" headache, that person is saying her head hurts like it is being split in two. It is not literally being split in two, but rather she is just trying to say that her head hurts terribly.

During March Madness (which by the way is figure of speech), fans will use many different figures of speech to describe the player who hit the game winning shot. Some would say that he was "clutch," that he had "ice-water in his veins," that he had "guts," and many other qualities conveyed in non-literal language. Other fans who hear these descriptions recognize all of these figures of speech immediately because they are used regularly to describe basketball players. Not a single listener would think that the player literally had ice water in his veins, but rather they understood that he was cool under pressure. ("Cool" is yet another figure of speech... See? We use them all the time!)

We will not always recognize the figures of speech that the biblical authors use right away, but we will recognize them faster when we pay attention to the context and ask ourselves the following questions: *Does the literal meaning of this word make sense in this sentence?* and *Is the author using a literary genre like poetry, prophecy, parables, puns?* We will also recognize them faster the more we read the Bible because the figures of speech will become a part of our vocabulary.

Action

Action draws us into stories and points us toward the meaning the author is conveying. The Bible is no different. The actions of God, either explicitly or implicitly, drive the arguments authors make in every genre of Scripture. Therefore, the careful reader should always pay close attention to who is doing what and what an important character says, particularly God, as he is revealed in the Father, the Son, and the Holy Spirit. This focus on the action will help us examine the verbs that are being used and determine what those actions reveal about the character of God or other important characters in the narrative.

Verbs carry the action. Paying attention to who acts and who receives the action can provide needed insight into the point an author is attempting to make in a passage of Scripture. Most of the time an author will be clear about who is doing what, but you may need to pay close attention to the pronouns an author uses while telling a story or making an argument. If the reader gets confused about which person the pronoun is representing, it will be unclear "who does and who receives" the action. Along with analyzing this *who does/who receives* question, a careful reader should pay attention to the voice of the verb.

I know... I know... I know... Please don't quit on me!

You might wonder why no one said that you would have to remember grammar to read the Bible! You might think this is why reading the Bible seems so hard. Grammar might not be fun, but understanding the Bible is so important that re-learning a little bit of grammar is worth it. The voice of a verb (active or passive) is not important, except when it is! The voice of a verb always helps us understand how an author is conveying his message, and many occasions exist where the voice of a verb only assists us in answering the *who does/who receives* question. Authors, however, can switch from the active voice (where the subject performs the action of the verb) to the passive voice (where the subject receives the action of the verb) to make a point. When that switch occurs, you should slow down to determine the point that the author is making.

Finally, why is this question so important? The actions that people (and God) perform reveal to the reader what an author is trying to convey about their character. When God saves or judges his people, we learn about his righteousness, covenantal love, and holiness. When people rebel against God we learn about their character and their need for a redeemer who will deliver them from their rebellion.

Phrases and Clauses

When I was a child, I enjoyed watching *School House Rock* while I watched Saturday morning cartoons. I learned about how a bill became a law and can still sing along, "I'm just a bill, a lonely ole bill, sittin' up on Capitol Hill..." I learned about adverbs in "Lolly, Lolly, Lolly, Get Your Adverbs Here." My favorite song, though, was *Conjunction Junction.* In that song, I learned that conjunctions have the role of "hookin' up words, phrases, and clauses"[6] and "and, but, and or, they'll get you pretty far." Who knew that this song would help me for the rest of my life as I read the Bible?

We use conjunctions in almost every sentence of every conversation we have and every email we write. We use them to make our intentions clear and to make a case for someone to agree with our opinions, but we fail to recognize that the biblical authors are doing the same thing. They are, particularly in the letters and the prophets, delivering a carefully constructed logical argument that could be declared publicly to a group of people who needed to hear the message, be persuaded by the message, and respond to the message. The verbs describe what people do, and the conjunctions help to explain how those actions are hooked together. We have already discussed the conjunctions that can be used with contrasts and comparisons, so now let's look at some others. This review will not be exhaustive but will explain some of the most important conjunctions for interpreting the Bible.

The most common types of conjunctions are coordinating conjunctions. You know, "they'll get you pretty far... and, but, and or" (we can also add so, yet, nor, and for). The other type of conjunction that we need to discuss is the subordinating conjunction. Paul, in particular, *loved, loved, loved* them (you might also say that I do), so we must *know, know, know* about them! These conjunctions establish logical relationships between clauses and help us to know *who, what, when, where, why, and how* the action of the main verb was done. Writers will answer the *who* and *what* questions with clauses that provide more information about nouns and explain traits that describe a character or idea. These types of conjunctions can be found in a sentence like the following: "The player, *who* hit the last second shot, caused the Wildcats to win the basketball game." The main adverbial clauses that we need to navigate are: temporal, causal, purpose/result, concessive, conditional, and means. These words might seem a bit dry, technical, and boring, but you use them every day. I just want you to recognize that Paul used them in the same way, and because of this similarity, you can understand what in the world he was talking about.

Let's look at the two following sentences. "The

Wildcats won the basketball game." "The player made the last-second shot."[7] The way that an author connects these two sentences makes a significant difference in what he or she is attempting to say in writing them.

- **Temporal** (*when, while, before, after, until*)
    - The Wildcats won the basketball game **after** the player made the last-second shot.
    - The Wildcats won the basketball game **when** player made the last-second shot.
- **Causal** (*because, for, since*)
    - The Wildcats won the basketball game **because** the player made the last-second shot.
- **Purpose/Result** (*that, in order that, so that, to + an infinitive*)
    - The player made the last-second shot **in order that** the Wildcats would win the basketball game.
    - The player made the last-second shot **with the result that** the Wildcats won the basketball game.
- **Concessive** (*even though, though, despite the fact that*)
    - The Wildcats won the basketball game **even though** the **Louisville** player made the last-second shot. (Notice here that the player's team had to change because of the type of clause we are illustrating.)

- **Conditional** (*if*)
  - **If** the player made the last-second shot, then the Wildcats would win the basketball game.
- **Means** (*by, through*)
  - The Wildcats won the basketball game **by** making the last-second shot.

Paying attention to these conjunctions will make your reading of the Bible more understandable and, therefore, more enjoyable.

TIME OUT: USING THE FIRST FIVE QUESTIONS

Let's pause for a minute, read our Bibles, and use these five techniques to make some observations about 1 John 1:5-2:2. As you read the passage, I would encourage you to create a symbol for each question, for instance a circle for repetition. As you mark the passage that you are studying, you will recognize quickly the observations that you have made. The observations below are not exhaustive, but they should give you an example of a process you can follow easily.

Repetition of Words and Themes

In 1 John 1:5-7, John uses "light" three times and "darkness" twice. Could this repetition be important when we interpret the passage? Additionally, John uses the terms "walk" and "fellowship" twice in 1:6-7. Throughout 1:8-2:2, John uses the noun for "sin" six times and the verb "to sin" twice. Clearly, this passage has much to say about sin. At this point, we do not know what it says about sin, but any summary of what the passage says must include a statement related to what John says about sin. In 1:5-10, John confronted his readers with the "truth" and the danger of "lies." On three occasions, John focuses on untruth by using the terms "to lie," "to deceive," and "liar." John uses the term "truth" on two occasions and continues the theme in 1:10 by asserting that God's word, which is truth, opposes ones who claim they have not sinned. Once we have completed our observations of repeated words and themes (and you may have found more than we have described here), we are ready to move on to the next technique.

Comparisons

When we examine the points of comparison that John presented in this passage, the reason for the repetition of themes becomes clearer. He begins by asserting that God is light and that no darkness can be found in him at all. Due to the fact that God is light and no darkness exists in him, John says that his readers should desire to be in the light and not in the darkness. John compares the lie that sin is and the lies that sin causes. Now, we recognize that John is using these terms to draw comparisons, but these comparisons become clearer when we observe that they define one central figure of speech in the passage.

Figures of Speech

The comparison that John makes between light and darkness brings us to a figure of speech he must explain. John asserts that God is light and in him is no darkness and that we can walk in the light as God is in the light and have fellowship with one another through the cleansing of sin that comes from Jesus. As a result, we must understand that "the light" is a figure of speech to describe the holiness and purity of God. Due to the "light" and "darkness" comparison that we have already noted, darkness must also be a figure of speech, which John uses to describe the sin of the people. We must then conclude that sin cannot exist in God's presence because his holiness will destroy it. When we bring all of our observations together, we must recognize the importance of this light and dark comparison—or figure of speech–because of its connection to the larger theme of sin (lies) and its opposition to the truth.

Action

This passage has the following five sets of characters: God (the Father), Jesus Christ (the righteous Son), us (John and his audience), John (the writer), and the children, (the letter's recipients). What does each of these groups do? First, John asserts that God is light and that darkness does not exist in his presence. As we move through 1:6-10, we must remember that John uses "he" and "his" to substitute for using the term "God" repeatedly. This means that not only does John asserts that God is light, but he also claims that God is faithful and just to forgive us of all our sin. John then concludes with the corollary that, if we say we have not sinned, we make God a liar and God's word is not in us.

In the course of the passage, John describes Jesus by referring to his sacrificial death that brought/brings cleansing for all sin, and he later describes Jesus as the Messiah, the Advocate, the Righteous One, and the propitiation for our sins. John also makes an amazing description of the great work that Jesus accomplished for his people through his death in which he bears the wrath of God and brings continued cleansing from sin. The only other place where Jesus seems to play an active role in this passage takes place in 1:5. In this verse, John asserts that Jesus is the one from whom they all heard the message that God is light.

The "we" play a prominent role in the passage. In using the first-person plural, John identifies with the recipients of the letter and admits that the truths, which he is presenting, are for all Christians. What actions do the "we" perform? The "we" say things like the following: "we have fellowship with him and we walk in darkness… we do not have sin… we have not sinned." All of these statements are conveyed in conditional clauses, which we will discuss in a moment, and are indicative of false statements that the "we" may be making. If "we" say these things, John claims, "we are lying and not practicing the truth… we are deceiving ourselves and the truth is not in us… we are making him [God] to be a liar and his word is not in us." Clearly, the "we" are in error, but John also presents a strong contrast for the "we." We whose sins have been cleansed by the blood Christ can walk with God and have fellowship with one another. If we confess our sins, God is faithful and just to forgive us and cleanse us from our unrighteousness. Finally, John declares that the "we" have an advocate with the Father, Jesus the Messiah, the Righteous One.

In 2:1, John provides one of several statements about his purpose for writing, like what he did in 1:4, John desires that the readers of this letter would recognize the seriousness of their sin and that they would not sin. He does, however, recognize that sin is an inevitability in life and that the atoning death of Jesus brings believers into right fellowship with God. John's description of the believers who received this letter as his children underscores the nature of his concern and could give insight into the tone of the letter. John writes as one who has great affection for these people and as one who desires to extend to them every spiritual protection possible to strengthen them for the journey of faith.

Phrases and Clauses

As we make our way through each verse, we must pay attention to what the subordinate clauses are and what they modify. In 1:5, John uses two subordinate clauses. The first, "which we have heard from him and are announcing to you," defines further the source of the message and what they are doing with it. The second clause, "that God is light and darkness is not in him, not any at all," provides the content of the message.

In 1:6, John employs the first of several conditional clauses that he uses to present both the truth and lies about sin in the life of the believer. He begins with the lie. Notice the repetition of the verb "say." Even though someone makes these claims, they are not the truth. In 1:7, John draws a contrast between the lie and the truth by using the coordinating conjunction "but." In 1:8, John returns to a conditional clause with the verb "to say" in order to present another lie that false teachers were perpetrating in this church. We again have a dependent clause describing the message of the false teachers. In 1:9, John again presents the contrast, as a conditional clause, where the confession of sin is tied to God being faithful and just in order to forgive us our sins and cleanse us from all unrighteousness. In 1:10, John employs one more conditional clause with a verb of "saying" followed by a dependent clause to provide for us the content of the lie that has been spoken. The result of this lie, which seems to be the culmination of the process of lying, is that one who speaks this lie asserts that God is a liar and can be described as one who does not know God at all.

In 2:1, John changes the structure of his argumentation as he begins a new paragraph. He shifts the argument and explains that he wrote this passage and this book to keep his readers from falling into sin. The conditional clause that follows recognizes that believers will sin and that Jesus is the atoning sacrifice for sin.

These observations bring us to the conclusion of stating the point that John was making to his readers in these paragraphs. I think that we could sum it up in the following, "God is holy and people are sinful. This reality means that sin in the life of a believer will hinder fellowship with God. So, pursue holiness recognizing that your fellowship with God is always grounded in the sacrificial death of Jesus."

The timeout is over. Let's finish up the last few questions. Game on!

Conversations

Look for quotation marks. When an author switches from presenting the things that people are saying indirectly (a summary) to giving a direct quotation of what the speaker said (a speech or conversation), pay careful attention. This switch is a clue that the author is emphasizing a key point. When studying a passage that is dominated by a conversation, ask some or all of the following questions to understand the point that the author is making: Who is talking? What is the tone of their conversation (friendly, confrontational, etc.)? Is there really a conversation happening? When questions are asked, does the person answer the actual question that was asked? If not, is the change important? Does the conversation reveal misunderstanding? All of these factors that present themselves as conversations take place provide important clues about what the author is trying to teach his readers through the way that he has told the story.

Take a moment to read Mark 4:35-41 carefully. As Mark tells the story, he introduces the nature of the excursion that Jesus and his disciples were taking to the other side of the Sea of Galilee. A great windstorm arose while they were out on the lake, and the boat was in great danger and was taking on much water while Jesus sleeps through the storm in the back of the boat. The disciples then woke Jesus up and asked him, "It does concern you that we are perishing, doesn't it?"[8] As we look at the question, we must ask ourselves about its tone. Is it kind and friendly? Are they concerned and frustrated? Mark continues, "After being awakened, Jesus rebuked the wind and said to the sea, 'Peace! Be Silent!'" To whom/what does Jesus speak? Does he speak to the disciples? Is Jesus afraid? Does he say anything mysterious? Do the wind and the sea obey?

After making this statement to the wind and the sea, Jesus turns and asks the disciples the following pointed question: "Why are you afraid? Do you not yet have faith?" What was the tone of this statement? Is there significance to the "not yet" statement? What was the response of the disciples as Mark recorded it? They said, "Who is this then that even the wind and the sea are obeying him?" Pay careful attention to the fact that Mark places this material in a quotation. This question is the central issue in every story in the Gospel of Mark. Who is Jesus? He is the Messiah, Son of God (Mark 1:1), whose identity is shown in this story by the authority he has over the wind and waves. He is doing things that only God can do.

Lists

This technique for understanding what an author is trying to say in a passage might energize some readers and sap the strength of others, but this technique plays an important role at various points in letters and speeches. Sometimes lists are straightforward like the comparison between the works of the flesh and fruit of the Spirit in Galatians 5 or the topic sentence for Luke's description of the church's expansion in Acts 1:8. On other occasions, the list might be subtler like the points that summarize a sermon. When the reader recognizes a list, writing the items on a separate piece of paper can be helpful because this activity makes seeing the number of items, similarities among items, differences among items, patterns in the listing items, and similarities to other lists in the Bible easier to see. Once the reader does this work, determining the author's purpose for including the list becomes a much simpler task to complete.

Take a moment to read Galatians 5:16-26. In this passage, Paul commanded the Galatians to walk by the Spirit in full confidence of the fact that doing so will lead them to live in such a way that they will not indulge in the works of the flesh. He made this claim in direct opposition to those in Galatia who argued that resisting the works of the flesh came through keeping the law, from which Paul has previously argued that Christ has freed them. He then moved into a list that compared the works of the flesh with the fruit of the Spirit. Let's compare the two lists to observe any patterns that arise.

Works of the Flesh	Fruit of the Spirit
Sexual immorality	
Impurity (Lewdness)	
Sensuality	
Idolatry	
Sorcery	
Hatred	Love
Strife	Joy
Jealousy (Zeal)	Peace
Anger	Patience
Contentious (Selfish)	Kindness
Division	Goodness
Factions	Faithfulness
Envy	Gentleness
Drunkenness	Self-Control
Carousing (orgies)	
Things like these	Against such things there is no law

When we examine the list that Paul has given to us, he has organized both of them to make the central point that the work of the Spirit in their daily lives as Christians is to promote and create love for one's neighbor that brings unity in the church. Notice the headings for each list. The works of the flesh correspond with the fruit of the Spirit. One group divides the body, and one unites it. Paul presents that reality subtly through the plural for the "works of the flesh" and singular for the "fruit of the Spirit." He then grouped the list around various types of works. The works of the flesh are sexual sins against one another, religious sins aimed at God, divisive sins against one another, and sins that demonstrate a lack of self-control. The fruit of the Spirit focus on the work that the Spirit does to foster unity in the body. As a result, when we look at Galatians as a whole, Paul confronted the church with the fact that the death of Jesus not only completed the promise of God to create for himself a family defined by faith in the promise of God, now revealed in Jesus and not the law, but also has resulted in the giving of the Spirit that empowers the people of God to live in a way that fulfills the command to love their neighbors as themselves. The law could not accomplish this reality.

Tone

Have you ever written an email where you offended someone because you were trying to portray one tone (like flattery or praise), but conveyed another (like sarcasm or mockery)? If so, you have recognized that the tone with which words are written is almost as important as the words themselves for communication to take place. Making tone come through on the written page is a tricky thing. Sometimes the biblical authors use strong, often figurative, words that produce emotion to create the tone they desire. These words can convey happiness, frustration, anger, and many other emotions. Notice how Matthew described Jesus' rebuke of the scribes and Pharisees when he called them hypocrites seven times in Matthew 23.

Authors use genres like poetry (Psalms) and prophecy (Revelation), which often use this figurative language, to produce emotions in their readers or to convey their own joy or sorrow. On other occasions, the author will provide a context where rather literal language can convey deeply held emotions. Paying attention to the emotional tone of a passage is important, but I would caution you to avoid manufacturing a tone because the authors frequently relate information in a rather straightforward fashion where no emotional tone is needed to interpret the passage.

CONCLUSION

Our goal in this chapter has been to slow down our pace of reading and to pay attention to the ways the biblical authors have constructed passages to convey the main point they were making. None of these observational techniques alone will give us a complete picture of what the main point of the passage is, but when we use all of them together (the ones that apply to the type of text we have before us), we can discern the point that an author was trying to convey. This work, however, does not end our quest. It is only the beginning. While a good portion of what we need to know about a passage can be discerned from a literary examination of it, understanding what the author was attempting to teach his original audience requires more work so that our arrows stay aimed in the right direction and hit our target.

ARROW 2:
WHAT DID THIS PASSAGE MEAN TO ITS ORIGINAL AUDIENCE?

←———

In our examination of Arrow 1, we focused on how to read the words on the page well. This careful reading typically provides us a basic understanding of the passage's meaning. As we examine the question "What did this passage mean to its original audience?" our focus will not be on gaining more meaning but on employing the tools that point us backward into the historical setting.

Using these tools to increase our knowledge about historical issues (like the audience and the authors) will sharpen our aim, increase the depth of our biblical understanding, and produce much spiritual fruit. Think of it this way: I (Donny) like red meat of just about any kind! When Bible readers seek to understand what the passage says, they are devouring a well-cooked and tasty cheeseburger that is filling, satisfying, and nourishing. If the only red meat you have eaten was a cheeseburger, you would think that red meat was great; however, suppose that at some point in your life you had the pleasure of eating a perfectly aged, perfectly prepared filet mignon. Once you have had that dining experience, you can still enjoy a cheeseburger and be satisfied, but the memory of the filet will still linger in your mind.

Similarly, the extra work to add depth to our understanding of God's word by employing tools to assist us in determining what the passage meant to the original audience results in an unrivaled experience of feasting on Scripture. We can continue to be nourished and satisfied by examining what the passage says, but, on some level, we will still want the added enjoyment and benefit that a greater depth of understanding can bring.

The journey toward understanding what a biblical text meant to its original audience can be frustrating and can seem filled with obstacles that block the path forward. Let's be honest, we've all heard preachers make reference to some obscure piece of historical information that seems crucial to understanding what a particular passage teaches. As a result, we just throw our hands up in the air and wonder why we are even trying.

Although I am in favor of learning as much as possible about the historical setting, the number of incidents where having obscure knowledge of a particular historical tidbit is absolutely necessary for understanding a passage's meaning is quite limited. Thankfully, some of the biblical authors even go out of their way to explain that helpful information in the text. Look at Mark 7:1-5 where Mark explains to his readers that the washing of the Pharisees is not an issue of sanitation but of religious ritual. Be encouraged because even the original recipients of the Bible did not understand some of this stuff and needed help! Gaining the amount of historical information that can be helpful to us is all about knowing what the right tools are and where to find them.

Having the right tools makes all the difference between success and failure in just about every endeavor in life. I am not handyman. In fact, I (and folks who have tried to help me!) would tell you that I am rather inept at most basic home improvement tasks. However, I have learned from my time as an electrical, carpentry, and plumbing assistant that the proper tools make seemingly impossible jobs rather manageable if you know how to use them. Another thing I have noticed during my "assisting" is that usually more than one tool can accomplish the task. Some have more bells and whistles than others, (like a cool laser that shows you where the saw blade is going to cut), but the more technical tool is not always the most helpful.

The tools for gaining the knowledge that will help point us in the right direction for understanding this Arrow are that. Some are technical and meant for professionals. Some use less jargon and convey the same information, accomplishing essentially the same result. Let me give you an example where I don't look as incompetent as I do in my handyman illustration.

When I was studying Mechanical Engineering at the University of Kentucky, I used a cheap, solar-powered, scientific calculator made by Casio. By the time I graduated, the metal face that showed what would happen when you used some of the scientific functions had fallen off. I believe that calculator cost less than $20. I had some classmates who spent well over $100 on their calculators, which could give a graphic display of an equation, unlike mine. Some of those calculators even had a weird, coded language that you had to learn to use them properly (kind of like the book of Revelation), but in the end my classmates and I all arrived at the same answer no matter which calculator (tool) we used.

So, let's talk about the tools that you need to determine what a biblical passage meant to its original audience. We need to know how to use the following tools in our tool belts: cross-references, maps, Bible dictionaries, New Testament and Old Testament surveys, and commentaries.[9]

CROSS-REFERENCES

Many Bibles will have either a column in the center, a section at the bottom, or a column on the side of the page where the editors of the Bible have made notations to link the terms or ideas in one verse with other passages of Scripture. These references can be helpful in learning how an author used a term throughout the book or books that he authored and in recognizing how an author (particularly a New Testament author) might have alluded to or quoted another biblical text (usually from the Old Testament) in order to convey a message to his readers.

These references generally fall into the following categories: references to specific words or phrases; comparative references, where the reader can find texts that have the same theme; indirect references, where the reader can find additional information about a theme that might expand upon the specific point made in the text; and direct quotations.[10]

Even though the connection between the biblical text you are studying and the cross-reference can sometimes be difficult to understand, the cross references are still an indispensable resource in the quest to understand what the author intended to say in a biblical text. To use an aiming analogy, with this tool you place the target in the sights on your bow so that your arrow will hit the target with more precision.

Suppose that you are having a difficult time understanding a word in the passage that you are studying. Maybe the term is the name of a place or a theological concept with which you are not familiar.

In this instance, a cross-reference might indicate locations where those terms occur elsewhere in Scripture. This added information could help clarify your understanding of the passage and the significance of that particular place in the biblical story or that particular theological concept.

Cross-references can also be helpful when you are studying the Gospels–particularly Matthew, Mark, and Luke–because they will indicate where the same story can be found in the other Gospels. At times, comparing the way that each author tells the story, particularly comparing Matthew and Luke with Mark, can assist you in understanding unique themes that an author is emphasizing in his telling of the story. Additionally, if the story is not found in another Gospel, you might pay extra close attention to the themes that arise in your reading of that text because the uniqueness of the story could point to a special emphasis by the author.

Finally, cross-references are most helpful when we examine how one author interprets another biblical text and draws out its implications for his readers. The authors of the books of the Bible were students of the Bible themselves and understood quite well that the Bible must be studied and applied to life. This fact should be a big encouragement to us as fellow students of Scripture and should enhance our appreciation of the interconnectedness of the entire biblical story.

The biblical writers make reference to texts written before their own time either through quotations or through allusions and draw upon the circumstances or the larger argument of the original text to deliver a dense theological message to their audience. As I said before, usually a New Testament author quotes or alludes to a passage from the Old Testament, but you should also look for references where the prophets in the Old Testament make to the Law. So, when cross-references point you to a text that comes before the one that you are studying (such as an Old Testament passage when you are studying the New), make sure to look at the larger context that surrounds the specific text to which the author is referring. This extra step will help make sense of why the author referenced a particular text and will provide depth to your study. Finally, if an author refers to several texts in a condensed area, take a step back to determine if these passages have an underlying theme that ties them together.

Let's look at Luke 2:22–35, a story that only occurs in this Gospel, and see how cross-references can provide depth to our understanding of what Luke is teaching his readers. Luke introduces this passage by explaining that "when the days of their purification were accomplished according to the Law of Moses," Joseph and Mary brought Jesus to the Temple to *present* or *dedicate* this firstborn son to the God. The first cross-reference in my Bible points me to Leviticus 12 where Moses records the instructions from God to remove the uncleanness of a woman that results from giving birth to a child. In Luke 2:24, Luke describes the specific sacrifice that Joseph and Mary performed, and the cross-reference again cites Leviticus 12. Luke's description of these events on the forty-first day of Jesus' life demonstrates to us that Jesus' parents were faithful to God's law not only in circumcising Jesus on the eighth day but also in performing the rite of ritual purification. Historically, the fact that Joseph and Mary used the sacrifice prescribed for poor Israelites provides us with evidence that the Magi (who are only mentioned in Matthew) have not yet arrived with their quite expensive gifts for the King of the Jews. (For this reason I won't let my wife place the Wise Men near the manger in our "historically accurate" nativity scene!)

Additionally, Luke describes Joseph and Mary as presenting Jesus to the Lord by explaining that every firstborn son in Israel is called "holy [separate] to the Lord" (2:23). The cross-reference points us to Exodus 13:2 and 13:12. In these texts, God commands Moses to have the people consecrate all of the firstborn in Israel. These children and animals belong to God and serve as a reminder of the fact that he saved them from his plague that killed the firstborn sons throughout Egypt. Following God's initial declaration that the firstborn sons and animals in Israel belong to him, Moses explained to the people that they must remember this great act of deliverance that God has performed through a celebratory feast. The consecration of firstborn sons and the celebration of remembrance would be of particular importance when they entered into the Promised Land because these actions would serve as a way to worship God by retelling the story of how he defeated Pharaoh, showed that his glory was greater than Pharaoh's, and demonstrated his faithfulness to Abraham, Isaac, and Jacob. Additionally, Luke uses this reference to the past deliverance of God in the Exodus to prepare the way for his references to the new exodus/restoration from the Exile[11] that Jesus would accomplish in fulfillment of the promises that God made through the prophets, particularly Isaiah.

In Simeon's prophetic word to Mary and Joseph (Luke 2:29–32), Luke records the following statement: "Master, now you are permitting your servant (to die) according to your word in peace because my eyes saw your salvation, which you prepared before the face of all peoples, a light for revelation for the nations and glory for your people Israel." Earlier in the passage (Luke 2:25), Luke explains that Simeon was waiting for the "consolation of Israel." The cross-references indicate that we should investigate Isaiah 40:1 and 57:18. Both texts describe the comfort that God will bring to his people when he delivers them from the Exile. In this prophetic speech to Mary and Joseph about what Jesus will do in the years to come, Simeon cites Isaiah's description of the way that God will restore his people after he judges them in the Exile. The cross-references point us to Isaiah 42:6, 49:6, 52:10, and 60:3.

In Isaiah 42:6, the prophet introduces his readers to the Servant of Yahweh whom God has chosen to lead his people out of the Exile, in whom God's soul delights, and upon whom God has placed his Spirit (look for these themes in Luke). The result of the work of the Servant will be not only the restoration of God's people but will also be a demonstration of God's glory to the nations. In Isaiah 49:6, the prophet explains again that the Servant will deliver Israel from the Exile and will bring salvation to the Gentiles. In Isaiah 52:10, we find a word of celebration and worship to God for the amazing salvation that he will bring to his people as he forgives them, returns them to the Promised Land, and demonstrates to the watching world that he alone is God, who reigns over all creation. Isaiah 60:3 reads as follows: "And nations shall come to your light, and kings to the brightness of your rising." This verse occurs in a prophetic exhortation to Israel to arise and rejoice in the work that God will do to recreate them and show them his glory again, but we must admit that this text may not have been alluded to by Luke as clearly as the other passages that we have examined. This final reference should help us to remember that the cross-references are not infallible but are helpful guides that can add depth to our understanding of one particular text and of how the whole biblical story fits together.

So, what is Luke telling us about Jesus? Luke is declaring that this little baby is the deliverer of Israel and the Gentiles who will believe in him as well. This fact would be clear without these references to Isaiah. But, by placing the messianic ministry that Jesus will have in the context of God's promise to restore his people from the Exile through the work of the Servant of Yahweh, Luke has demonstrated in a compelling way that Israel's God reigns over history, keeps his promises, has revealed himself ultimately in this little baby that Simeon is holding in his arms, and, along with Simeon's words about a sword piercing Mary's soul, foreshadows the way that this deliverance will be established (Isa 52:13–53:12).

MAPS

Preachers often joke that they believe the Bible is the inspired, inerrant word of God from Genesis to the maps! Sadly, this proclamation of belief is typically the only mention that the maps in your Bible receive. While pinpointing exactly where an event in the Bible happened is not fundamentally necessary to understanding what an author was teaching about that particular event, knowing where something happened provides geographical context and local color to our reading of the Bible that will enhance the vividness of our visualization of the events that we are studying and will confirm the truthfulness of historical claims that the Bible makes. Additionally, the location where an event takes place can also give us an understanding as to why certain things happen in one place but not in others.

Let's look at an example from the Gospel of Mark. While Mark emphasizes the hidden nature of Jesus' Messiahship to show that a complete understanding of who he was could not be discerned until he died as one forsaken by God, Jesus also had his own historical reasons for keeping his identity quiet. Have you ever wondered why Jesus would command certain people to keep quiet about receiving a healing and would command others to proclaim what he had done freely? Compare the healing of the man possessed with Legion to the raising to life of Jairus' daughter. In Mark 5:1–20, Jesus provides an awesome demonstration of his power by casting out Legion, but notice what happens next. The formerly demon-possessed man wanted to follow Jesus onto the boat and back across the lake so that he could be with Jesus, but Jesus did not allow it. Instead, he commanded the man to go to his own house and family and to proclaim to them "as many things as the Lord has done for you and shown you mercy." Mark summarizes the man's work, "and he departed and began to preach in the Decapolis as many things as Jesus did, and all were marveling" (5:20).

Contrast that story with Mark 5:21–43. Mark presents the stories of the raising of Jairus' daughter and the healing of the woman with the issue of blood. For our purposes, let's examine the conclusion of the story in 5:41–43. After enduring the mockery of the crowd, Jesus enters the room, takes her by the hand, and simply tells her to wake up. Understandably, the people in the room with him were amazed when she wakes up. Then, Jesus tells them to tell no one what they had seen.

Why does Jesus deal with these two healings so differently? In the first miracle story, Jesus has ventured to the eastern side of the Sea of Galilee (which we can only know from looking at a map even in this instance where the exact location of the town is not clear) and entered the region of the Decapolis. In the second story, Jesus has crossed back over the sea into Galilee. Why does this matter? The Decapolis was a region inhabited largely by Gentiles where declaring openly that Jesus was the Messiah would not create much controversy. Making this same claim in Galilee would make folks think Jesus had come to defeat the Romans with military might and could have caused people to start a revolt (See also Mark 1:43-45; 3:7-12; 7:31-37; 8:22-26 9:2-9; where Jesus commands silence in Jewish territories).

Purchasing a good Bible Atlas will enhance your knowledge of the region in which the events recorded in the Bible took place even beyond what the maps in your Bible can provide because atlases have more detailed maps and vivid pictures that help you visualize the land and terrain where the events took place. Take note of Carl Rasmussen's introduction to the *Zondervan Atlas of the Bible*:

> *This atlas has been written in the belief that once one has a basic understanding of the geography of the Middle East, one has a much better chance of coming to grips with the flow of historical events that occurred there. This is not to say that the physical environment dictated the events of history; nevertheless, it should be recognized that historical events were oftentimes greatly influenced by the geographical environments in which they occurred.*[12]

This resource can help awaken the reader's ability to imagine what took place and how events happened in the biblical narrative and can serve as a conduit to understanding what the biblical author wanted to teach his readers.

BIBLE DICTIONARIES

Have you ever been confused by words that show up in the Bible? Have you ever wanted an overview of every event in the Bible that took place in a certain location?

Did you ever wonder what that place looks like today, and what a map of the city in Bible times could have looked like? Have you ever wanted a brief overview of a book of the Bible that you are about to study? Have you ever wanted an overview of the life of a character that you read about? Have you ever been puzzled by a theological term that you have read in a book or heard in a sermon?

A quality Bible dictionary could help us find the answers to all of these questions and many more. While other resources exist that contain this kind of information, Bible dictionaries provide great help because they compile a variety of material, many times in one volume, and present it in a succinct and digestible fashion.

Let's look at a couple of examples from the Gospels. First, we will examine how a Bible dictionary can give us a simple definition to a word that we might not know. Second, we will consider the background information that a Bible dictionary can give us about a Jewish Festival that will bring clarity and depth to our reading of a story from the Gospel of John.

In Mark 6:30–44, Mark tells the story of Jesus feeding five thousand men, along with women and children, through the multiplication of five loaves and two fish. When Jesus tells the disciples to give the crowd something to eat, the disciples respond with the question, "After going into town, could we buy two hundred denarii worth of bread and give them to eat?" In this context, *denarii* seem to be some type of money, but the author does not tell us anything else to clarify how much. Depending on exactly how difficult it was to earn *denarii*, the sentence could either be an expression of their ability to accomplish the task or of their complete inability to do so. In a Bible dictionary, you could determine that the term, *denarii*, is the plural form of *denarius*, which is the equivalent of the money received by an ordinary laborer as a day's wage (essentially this amount was equivalent to more than 60% of a year's salary). You might even find an accompanying picture showing what one looked like.[13] Clearly, this knowledge about a denarius is not necessary to understand the main point that Mark is making—that Jesus is the Messiah, the Son of God who has authority from God to multiply the food and shepherd his people. But, it enhances the vividness Mark's description and makes our reading more enjoyable.

In John 7–8, Jesus makes his way to Jerusalem for the Feast of Booths and declares on the last day of the feast that anyone who is thirsty can come to him and drink (John 7:37–38) and that he is the light of the world (John 8:12). In the first instance, John explains that Jesus' statement about providing water for the thirsty was a promise that Jesus would give the Spirit to those who believed in him. In the second assertion (John 8:12), John builds upon the contrast in his Gospel between the light and the darkness to demonstrate that Jesus is the Messiah, Son of God who is overcoming the evil world (John 1:9-13). However, could we deepen our understanding of John's message if we learn more about the Feast of Booths?

In the *Holman Illustrated Bible Dictionary*, the article on the Feast of Booths provides a summary of information about the festival as it was instituted in the Law and how it was practiced in the Jesus' day. While you might find it odd for the Jewish people to celebrate the era in which they wandered in the wilderness due to their rebellion against God, the celebration, which also included thanks to God for the fall harvest, was a reminder of God's gracious provision for his people during this time of punishment. On the first day of the festival, the participants made booths in which they lived throughout the feast. For the purposes of understanding our passage, the article goes on to explain that during Jesus' day rituals related to water and light were practiced as part of the celebration. Each day, priests drew water from the Pool of Siloam and poured it out on the altar, and at night, they lit massive menorahs (candelabras) to shine light on the Temple.[14] This information provides added weight to the statements that Jesus makes during the festival because he is setting himself up as the true presence of God, who is greater than the festival and the Temple itself. Jesus is not only the true King and final deliverer of his people, but he is also God in the flesh. Having this additional information from a Bible dictionary can enhance our knowledge of what the historical audience might have seen and understood when Jesus spoke these words and John wrote them.

I recognize that many of you might not want to purchase a Bible dictionary right away and would prefer to use a free tool on the web. First, be wary of historical information that you find on the Internet. Do not trust Wikipedia![15] Here are a few websites that could be of benefit to you: biblestudytools.com (Baker and Easton) and studylight.org (use Holman[16] and Baker).[17] Most of the Bible dictionaries that are available for free on the web are dated or have been replaced by updated versions but should be helpful on most occasions. Second, while I love my Kindle for books like *Seven Arrows*, I am a bit old school and prefer hard copies of my Bible dictionaries, and I think that you will too.

SURVEYS OF THE OLD AND NEW TESTAMENT

Surveys give an overview of both the background information (author, date of composition, setting, etc.) as well as an overview of a book in the Bible's contents. A brief version of what I am referring to can be found at the beginning of each book in a good study Bible, but it is usually only a paragraph or two long. However, book-length surveys provide much more detailed and helpful information about each book of the Bible.

Surveys of the Old and New Testament are an indispensable tool to assist the Bible reader in gaining a deeper understanding of the individual books of the Bible. They can also offer insight about the cultural world in which these works were penned, the process that resulted in the recognition of the fact that these books were inspired by God, and the methods used by scholars to study these books. When you begin the study of a particular book of the Bible, reading the survey entry about that book will provide a big picture view that has more detail about the narrative flow of the book and its theological themes than could be found in a Bible dictionary. This type of information will help the reader gain a better familiarity with the whole of the book. Keep in mind that, as we saw in our investigation of Arrow 1, interpreting an individual passage demands that you not only have a grasp on what the author was teaching in the sections that immediately surround your passage but also on what his purposes were in the book as a whole.

Additionally, surveys can provide a big picture view of the theological, political, and social setting in which these books were written. In the New Testament, this information is extremely helpful because of the theological and political turmoil in Galilee and Judea from the end of the time period covered by the Old Testament up to the time that John the Baptist comes onto the scene. Surveys can also help us understand the conflict of worldviews that took place as the Christians proclaimed the good news of Jesus and his Kingdom to both Jews and pagans.

Finally, these surveys can provide a glimpse into the methodologies that scholars have used throughout the history of the church in their efforts to understand what the biblical authors were trying to teach their audiences. While the incorrect application of these methods (sometimes driven by anti-Christian presuppositions) by some scholars had quite negative results, learning about the tools themselves could sharpen one's ability to dig into the message of the Scriptures.

COMMENTARIES

Commentaries provide a much more detailed look at the big picture information covered in a survey and will also include a *careful* explanation of each passage in a book. Sometimes, diving into a commentary can be intimidating. Typically, a commentary should be used as a reference book and should not be read from cover-to-cover apart from your own study of the Bible itself. Commentaries should be used as a tool to add depth to your study of individual passages. Commentaries also serve as a safety net to protect us from falling into interpretive error. To draw on our aiming analogy again, commentaries keep us from missing the target altogether and hitting an unsuspecting bystander with our arrow.

Whenever you start studying a particular book of the Bible, I would encourage you to pick up a commentary or two that will assist you in your attempts to determine what the original author was attempting to teach the original audience. Even after completing a PhD in New Testament, I would never prepare to teach a book study at North Greenville University or to preach a sermon without supplementing and checking my own study with a few commentaries. I do, however, want to warn you against the temptation to depend on the commentary rather than reading the Bible itself. Commentaries are exceedingly helpful, but they are not inerrant and will never be a substitute for actually reading, studying, struggling with, and meditating upon the biblical text.

Let's look at an example of how a commentary can give us even more historical information about an event than is possible in a Bible dictionary or survey. In our discussion of Bible dictionaries, we examined how understanding the way that the Jews practiced the Feast of Booths during Jesus' day could aid our understanding of Jesus' claims that he is the Water of Life and the Light of the World. Listen to the more detailed description of the water ceremony that Gary Burge gives in his commentary on the Gospel of John:

Each day of the feast witnessed a water ceremony in which a procession of priests descended to the

south border of the city to the Gihon Spring (which
flowed into the Pool of Siloam). There a priest filled a
golden pitcher as a choir chanted Isaiah 12:3: "With
joy you will draw water from the wells of salvation."
The water was then carried back up the hill to the
"Water Gate," followed by crowds carrying a lulab
in the right hand (tree branches reminiscent of
the desert booths) and an ethrog in the left hand
(citrus branches reminiscent of the harvest). The
crowd would shake these and sing Psalms 113-118.
When the procession arrived at the temple, the
priest would climb the altar steps and pour the
water onto the altar while the crowd circled him
and continued singing. On the seventh day of the
festival, this procession took place seven times.[18]

Before we attempt to unpack the significance of this historical detail in our interpretation of these passages, let's read what type of historical information stands behind Jesus' statement that he is the Light of the World. Burge explains,

The Mishnah (the recorded tradition of the Rabbis
on the practice of the Law) chapter on Tabernacles
(Sukkah) provides lavish descriptions of both the
water and light ceremonies and explains that
whoever has not seen these things has never seen
a wonder in his or her life! Four large stands each

*held four golden bowls; these were placed in the
heavily-used Court of the Women. These sixteen
golden bowls (reached by ladder) were filled with
oil and used the worn undergarments of the priests
for wicks (m. Sukkah 5). When they were lit at night
(so the rabbis said), all Jerusalem was illumined.
In a world that did not have public lighting after
dusk, this light shining from Jerusalem's yellow
limestone walls must have been spectacular.
Choirs of Levites would sing during the lighting
while "men of piety and good works" danced in the
streets, carrying torches and singing hymns.*[19]

Again, we have received some fascinating and disturbing historical information (the burning of undergarments) that places the statements of Jesus within a historical context. This context could provide added punch to the statements that Jesus was making to his audience, and John is now using them to accomplish his purpose of describing Jesus as the Messiah, Son of God.

As we previously learned, this festival had the purpose of reminding the children of Israel of the way that God graciously provided for them as they wandered in the wilderness. It was a living, dramatic presentation of their history. But, it also served as a picture of their hope that God would intervene on their behalf to save them in a way that exceeded the Exodus (16:14-15).

Given this context, references to "water" in the Old Testament then can inform our reading of the passage. First, the water ceremony pictured the miracle that God worked to provide them water in the desert from the rock, but the other side of the coin was Israel's accusation that God had forgotten his covenant and brought them into the wilderness to die preceded both occasions where this miracle took place (Exod 17:1-7; Num 20:2-13). Additionally, multiple prophets used this image of water from God (symbolized in the Temple) to describe the great salvation that God would bring to pass when he forgave their sins and ended the Exile (Isa 12:1-5; Ezek 47:1; Zech 14:8).[20] So, when Jesus stands up and declares that the thirsty should come to him and that those who believe in him would have rivers of living water flowing from out their bellies, he is declaring that he is greater than the Temple, the conjunction of heaven and earth, God in the flesh, and that the salvation to which this festival points comes through believing in him! John explains this statement to his readers further by stating that Jesus made this reference to water in order to describe the giving of the Spirit, which the prophets described would be a result of God's work of redemption to end the Exile (Isa 32:15, 43:16-44:5; Ezek 11:14-21, 36:22-32, 37:11-14, 39:21-29; Joel 2:28-29). John goes on to explain that this giving of the Spirit would take place after Jesus was glorified. Later, John will explain that this glorification will be Jesus' death and resurrection.[21]

Now, let's consider how the setting of the feast informs John's interpretation of Jesus' statement that he is the "Light of the World." Historically, the pilgrims in Jerusalem looked forward to the lighting of the lamps each night as the sun was going down. This part of the celebration had its roots in the Exodus narrative and was a celebration of the gracious way that God had brought them through the wilderness wanderings with a pillar of fire by night and served as a way for the Jews to worship God through remembering the grace that he had lavished upon them in the past.[22] In this setting, Jesus declares, "I am the Light of the World, the one who follows me will not walk in darkness but will have the light of life" (John 8:12). Through Jesus' statements here, John explains that Jesus was and is God in the flesh and is the light who will transform this evil world. As a result, believing in Jesus is the way to know God and to receive life, not the Temple or its rituals.[23]

Remember that commentaries can provide lots of useful information that can offer a more robust understanding of a particular passage. Use them wisely as you study, but never let them become a substitute for reading God's word.

CONCLUSION

These five tools can add depth to our understanding of how the passage that we are studying connects to other texts in the biblical story (cross-references), what was happening in the historical narratives of the Bible (maps), or how historical-cultural information about when and where something was written or about how customs that might be strange to us might impact our understanding of a passage (dictionaries, surveys, and commentaries). However, they are *not* a substitute for our use of the reading techniques that we examined in chapter one because those methods will help us to engage the inspired Scripture ourselves. The information that these tools can bring can be fascinating, but I beg you to avoid becoming so dependent on these tools that you forget to read the Scripture itself, because the Scripture alone is the inspired word of God! Finally, none of the information that I have presented in this chapter should cause you to study the Bible in isolation. After using these tools, Matt and I would still encourage you to seek godly counsel from fellow believers in the church and, most importantly, your pastors. Your pastors have been tasked with teaching you and keeping watch over your souls and desire to come alongside of you and assist you in setting the sights on your bow so that this arrow can be aimed in the right direction.

ARROW 3:
WHAT DOES THIS PASSAGE TELL US ABOUT GOD?

How many times have you heard people say that they just can't understand what the Bible is teaching? I (Donny) am convinced that many folks struggle to understand the Bible because they are trying to unlock what the Bible is teaching with the wrong key. They believe the key to the story is *me*, when the key is realizing that every story is about *God*. So, they are trying to unlock the door to understanding the Bible with a key that will never accomplish the task. So, what causes us to misread the story in this way?

I think two reasons stand out above all the rest. First, we are sinful, self-centered people, who believe that everything thing in the story of the Bible revolves around us. Second, we do not understand the story of the gospel or its goal. The gospel declares the kingship of Jesus and the kingdom that he established in his death and resurrection. It is not about us. Additionally, the forgiveness that comes through believing in Jesus is not the goal of salvation but the means to the greater prize of being reconciled with and knowing God.[24] So, Christian life becomes an epic quest to know our great king not a tweet about being forgiven and avoiding hell.

Compare this quest with my desire to my wife more each day. When we entered into this covenant relationship, I knew a lot about Amber, and she knew a lot about me. I did not, however, know everything about who she is and what makes her tick. After more than a decade, I still don't, but I will spend the rest of my life trying to know her better because I want to love her well (Eph 5:25-33).

When we are converted, we at least have to know something about God's work in Christ, but we don't really know *him*. The Bible allows us to move beyond just knowing what God has done to save us–to learn about God and his mission to fix the brokenness of the world. Salvation changes our story from one of alienation in sin to adoption in Christ. Being known by God (Gal 4:8-9) and being brought into the story of his work to restore the brokenness of all creation frees us to live out his mission in local churches and causes us to understand that he is at the center of every Bible story.

The whole Bible displays the relationship that God establishes with his blessed people. In the legal portions of Scripture, God graciously provides Israel with the Law to govern the relationship he had established in the promise he made to Abraham. He gave the Law so that they could understand that he alone is God, that he is perfect in his character and actions, and that he is gracious to provide a means for this sinful people to commune with him. The Psalms declare the worshipful response of God's people to his greatness, goodness, and loving-kindness to them. The Proverbs describe God's wisdom for living in a way that exalts his name. The prophets declare that God fights zealously for the hearts of his people, that God protects his justice by judging them, and that God will restore them after the judgment because he never breaks his promise—not even when his people break theirs. In the New Testament letters, the writers explain what God has done in Christ to fulfill his promises and extend his blessing to the nations. In Revelation, God completes the story by restoring his creation and eliminating Satan, sin, and death from it.

As we investigate the larger biblical story, we are turning the key for unlocking the door to understanding every passage in the Bible. You might wonder how that can be true. For those of us living in the 21st century, the story of the Bible could only be seen when the sixty-six books were brought together in one collection.[25] Now that these books have been brought together, we can see God's amazing plan from creation to new creation on full display. We must recognize, however, that the people of God in the Bible understood themselves to be living out the story of God's work to redeem his creation. Because God had chosen them to be his people, his story was their story, and it needed a proper ending. Jesus was just that.

We will divide the Bible's story into the following four parts: *The King's Reign*, *The King's Judgment*, *The King's Return*, and *The King's Reign*.

THE KING'S REIGN

In Genesis 1-2, Moses declares that God reigns over the whole creation and provides us a glimpse of his purpose for creating. God fashioned humans in his image, separating them from the rest of the creation, and blessed them. This creation is perfect because its creator is perfect. The culminating verse of Moses' big picture description of creation reads: "And God saw everything that he had made, and behold, it was very good. And there was evening and there was morning, the sixth day" (Gen 1:31). Everything God made performed the function for which God made it. Humans lived freely and openly before God and knew a peace and harmony with God that our words cannot describe fully.

Throughout the creation story, we observe that God, the creator King, created humans to bear his image and to live in communion with him. The blessing of God's presence came with God's command to have children and to extend his reign throughout the perfect world that God had made by acting as his stewards. Along with these responsibilities to extend God's reign, came one prohibition. Do not eat the fruit from the tree of the knowledge of good and evil because when you eat from it you will die (Gen 2:15-17).

When Adam and Eve rebel in the garden by attempting to overthrow his rule, God judges both them and the whole creation over which they ruled. Because God is the sovereign, faithful, and holy king, no created thing will ever thwart his plan or surprise him. So, we should not be surprised when he responds to this act of rebellion with judgment and a plan. God promises to provide one from the seed of the woman who will crush the serpent's head, recreate his people, and restore their communion with God so that they can worship him rightly and extend his reign (Gen 3:15-20).

THE KING'S JUDGMENT

After an unbelievably great beginning, rebellion saturates the next part of the story. In Genesis 3, Moses recounts humanity's fall into sin as Adam and Eve disobeyed God's command against eating from the tree of the knowledge of good and evil and rebelled against his reign in their desire to be *like* God. The result of this rebellion against God's rule shattered their communion with him. They now feared the presence and faced the punishment of God, but this blatant rebellion against God's kingship demonstrates that God will accomplish his purpose in and through his people even as he judges them. The curses placed upon Adam and Eve reveal that God's commands remain intact, but these commands, rather than being a delight, will be drudgery. Additionally, God's model for flourishing in their marriage will be a source of frustration instead of freedom. Finally, God ejects them from the Garden (from his presence) but graciously protects them by cutting off their access to the Tree of Life because eating from that tree while under God's curse would place them and their offspring under his eternal judgment.

God establishes the trajectory for the rest of the story in Genesis 1-3. He reigns over his creation before and after humanity's rebellion and graciously judges his people to magnify his perfect holiness (separateness from sin). God also extends his unfailing love as he prepares a way for their fellowship with God to be restored through the defeat of sin and death. As you read the Bible and use the *Seven Arrows*, you will find these twin foundations of God's character on display throughout the story. This repetition serves to convict us of the sin that separates us from the holy God and to remind us of our need for his amazing, unwavering grace.

Now that the foundational elements of the story have

been established, get ready for some amazing twists and turns as God works to restore this rebellious people. The amazing thing about this thrill ride is that God established its twists and turns even and how it would turn out before he created the world. Even though God's people sometimes thought this story was some kind of choose-your-own-adventure book, please don't ever be so foolish as to view his sovereign plan in this way.

In the next several chapters of Genesis, we find that rebelling against God's kingship motivated almost every thought and action of humanity. Therefore, God responds in judgment again. Noah, however, found favor with God. He was righteous and blameless, and he walked with God (Gen 6:5-9). God communes with Noah, blesses him initially through sparing his family from the judgment of the flood, and gives them the command of being fruitful and filling the earth to extend God's reign throughout the earth, just God commanded Adam and Eve (Gen 6:11-9:17).

The apex of rebellion against God's rule in Genesis 1-11 transpires in the debacle at Babel. In this story, the people decide to settle in one place so that they would not be spread out over all the earth and to build a tower so that they could make a name for themselves. They were saying to God that he was not King and that his rule was not wanted or needed. So, God judged them by confusing their speech and dispersing them to show them who *really* was king.

At this point, the story takes a shocking turn because God chooses to bless the world through a family that has zero children and no hope for any. This peculiar choice will show once again that God rules over his creation and will accomplish his purposes out of the ashes of judgment. He alone is God. He alone is King. He alone deserves credit for blessing his people with his presence!

God Chooses Abraham's Family

Until Genesis 12, God has commanded his people to be fruitful, multiply, and fill the earth. When God calls Abram, everything changes. As the preceding chapters have demonstrated, the fall has marred all of creation. Due to of sin, no one has the ability to keep God's commands, yet God promises to employ Abram and his family to bring his blessing to the world. Promise replaces command. God will transform this family, made up of an old man and an old, barren woman, into a great nation. He even promises to make their name great (contrast this statement with Babel).

Are you stumped about how God is going to accomplish his purpose of blessing *all* the families of the earth through this family? You should be! God chose them because they were the least of all the peoples of the earth so that he could show his power as King (Deut 7:6-11). You would at least think that God would give them a child quickly, but he doesn't.

After a few years pass (and still no baby), God appears to Abram in a vision and declares that he is Abram's shield and his reward will be great. In this encounter, God reaffirms his promise by declaring that Abram's own son will be his heir. Abram believed God, and God credited this belief to him as righteousness. Notice here that God alone declares who possesses a right status with him and that the status comes by believing God's promise. God then ratifies the covenant through a ceremony in which he, through the images of the smoking fire pot and flaming torch, walks through the dead animals, signifying that if he did not keep this promise he would die like the animals (Gen 15:1-21).

Finally, in Genesis 17, nearly twenty-five years after the initial promise, God reaffirms the covenant and declares that Abram and Sarai will have the child of the promise within the next year. This child of promise, whom God calls Isaac, will be the one whose descendants will bring God's blessing to the world. But, how does this tiny family become a great nation that will carry God's blessing to the nations?

Genesis concludes with Jacob, Isaac's son of promise, and his family (around 70 people) in Egypt under the protection of the one, true God. Pay close attention to what the Joseph (one of Jacob's sons but not the son of promise) story tells the reader about the greatness and omnipotence of God. In a world where most cultures believed that a god's power extended only as far as their nation's borders, the God of Abraham, Isaac, and Jacob is not only in control of Canaan, but he is also in control of Egypt. He is the sovereign King. This conclusion sets the stage for the destruction of the Pharaoh, whose people worshiped him as a god.

Before we move forward, maybe reading the Old Testament has been the source of a lot of frustration for you. I get it. That world is so different from ours. The rituals are strange, and keeping the Hivites separate from all the other –ites seems impossible. We can minimize these road blocks if we always keep in mind that God is using these events and people and rituals as road signs to remind us that this journey is headed to an amazing climax in which God will complete his plan to destroy sin and death and fill the earth with his glory. As you answer the question posed by Arrow 3, keep returning to this storyline. In time, you will find that the complexity and detail of God's plan will turn from drudgery to delight (and don't forget to use the cross-references).

God Saves His People

Notice how the book of Exodus begins. God has kept his promise while the Israelites were in Egypt. They have been fruitful, have multiplied, and have filled the Land. Trouble arises, however, when a king "who did not know Joseph" ascends to the throne. He recognizes that they are being blessed with many children and are becoming strong, so he conceives of various plans to destroy their fruitfulness. He makes them slaves. He plots to murder male children, but God thwarts his plans because the midwives feared God more than Pharaoh. God then works in a miraculous fashion so that a Hebrew boy, Moses, would grow up in the Pharaoh's palace and then lead his people to freedom.

In Exodus 3, God calls Moses to be the leader of the people by appearing to him in a bush that was on fire but not being consumed. In this encounter, God reveals his name to Moses and tells him to declare to the people that the Lord has sent him. When God says, "I AM WHO I AM," he is expressing his eternality along with his sovereignty as he again acts in a place where other gods supposedly reigned. God assures Moses that the people will listen to him and also commands him to go to the king of Egypt to demand that he release God's people. God promises to plunder Egypt and release them from slavery so that his sovereign rule over Egypt's gods and their king be clear. As the narrative unfolds, God does everything that he said he would do.

These truths should *leap* off of the pages of Scripture. God *always* does what he promises to do! He is faithful. As you read the Bible and learn how the passage aims you answer to Arrow 3, consider how your heart should be prompted to worship God, who unlike us, does exactly what he says he will do and exactly what is right in every circumstance. This truth should give you hope no matter how awful the circumstance—a broken marriage, a wayward child, or an uncertain future. God is not only faithful but also in control.

God takes Israel out of Egypt and places her on a course to complete the journey that Abraham had begun many generations before. When Israel reaches Sinai (Exod 19), God provides instruction to Moses through which he will make provision so that this sin-filled people can dwell near to this holy God. First, God reminds Israel of the fact that he made them his people and that he had acted to carry them out of Egypt. This history lesson underlines the fact that the God of Israel is the only God, is all-powerful, and keeps his covenant (a fact they often forget). They must also remember that this law did not make them God's people. God in his grace made them his own and now provides instruction about how to commune with him in safety for he is a consuming fire. Finally, this passage also provides for us a picture of the ferocity of God's holiness and how it destroys sin and the sinful.

Note again how the two foundational themes of God's gracious love and his holiness appear again at this pivotal moment in the biblical story. As the story unfolds, God declares that he will and speaks to them directly so that they will believe his instruction, but to hear this word, the people have to purify themselves to be that close to God.

God also commands that boundaries should be set so that this people (who are still sinful even with the preparation to be clean before God) will not come too close to him, because God is still distinctly different from his people. He is untouched and untainted by sin. In fact, violators of this boundary must be stoned or shot with an arrow (ironically!) and not even touched by his people (Exod 19:1-25).

When the day of God's visitation comes, the mountain is covered with a thick cloud, accompanied by thunder and lightning, and then God descends in fire. God makes gracious provision for Moses and Aaron to go beyond the boundary to act as intermediaries between God and the people, and, even here, God gives a warning that no one else can come up on the mountain. Then, God speaks the Ten Commandments, and the people are terrified by the awesomeness and holiness of the God who speaks in thunder. These commands underline again that God is their savior, is the only God, demands undivided loyalty from them, is too majestic to be caricatured in an idol, judges covenant breakers, blesses covenant keepers, and must be revered (Exod 20:18-26).

This awesome display of God's power, greatness, and demands should overwhelm us with awe! Notice, however, the first statement about God. He was their *savior*! As the story of Israel unfolds and the individual instructions are presented, don't ever forget that God was their *savior*. God has always been in the process of creating a holy people who carry God's blessing to the nations. I don't want to give away too much of the ending of the story, but God is doing the same thing in the New Testament. In fact, every word of Scripture is God's gracious instruction for our flourishing and never arbitrary demands from an angry God.

As the story continues to unfold, God remains faithful to his promises as he leads them on this journey to the Land that he promised Abraham even as Israel rebels against his kingship and accuse him of bringing them into the wilderness to die. Eventually, God leads them to the borders of the Promised Land and commands them to send spies into the Land. Just as God promised, this good land was fertile and flowing with milk and honey (Num 13:25-33). Sadly, the people forget that God is their savior and rebel against his kingship because they doubt his ability to conquer the cities of this land. In response, Joshua and Caleb rebuke the people for their rebellion and lack of faith, and then God's glory appeared at the Tent of Meeting (Num 14:1-4).

As Moses begs God to spare these rebels, he emphasizes several attributes of God that must dominate our understanding of who he is. Moses first describes the *power* of God to deliver his people in the Exodus and then explains that God *dwells* among his people. This combination of *power* and *proximity* makes the God of Israel unique among the gods of the other nations. He continues by comparing the *justice*, *mercy*, *faithfulness*, and *glory* of God to demonstrate how these attributes work together within the unchanging, holy character of God. God will not allow rebellion to go unpunished. So in his justice, the adults who saw God's glory and signs in Egypt and in the wilderness, with the exception of Joshua and Caleb, will receive exactly what they asked for—death in the wilderness. Their children, the very ones that they feared the Canaanites would slaughter, will possess the Land. So, a death march in the wilderness begins. During those forty years, God will repeatedly show his power and faithfulness to his people so that, quite ironically, when Israel camps at the Jordan River and prepares to enter the Land the Canaanites will quake in fear (Josh 2:8-14). Everywhere Yahweh takes Israel is his territory, and they know their land is next!

God Conquers for His People

Before his death, Moses exhorts the people to remain true to the covenant once they enter the Promised Land so that they make the goodness and greatness of their God known to the nations. Once Joshua begins to lead the people, God divides the waters of the Jordan River, leads them into the Land, and triumphs over their enemies. As the stories of Jericho (Josh 6) and Ai (Josh 7) demonstrate, Israel (and we) must never forget that God—not the

Israelite army—is conquering the Land. When the conquest narrative concludes, Joshua reminds the people that God gave them peace and prosperity in the Land that he had promised to Abraham, but he echoes the ominous warning from Moses' farewell address is echoed in his last words as well (Josh 24:14-28). Joshua then exhorts the people to put away their idols and choose this day to serve the Lord, and they commit to follow him. This commitment would not last.

God Remains Faithful to His People

Joshua (just like Moses) knew that they would be unable to keep their promise, and the narrative of Judges demonstrates that fact clearly and repeatedly. Judges is characterized by a repetitive cycle of sin, exile, repentance, restoration, and rest. During this cycle, God demonstrates his holiness by judging his people for their sin causing their enemies to oppress them and around the Land and his faithfulness to the Abrahamic covenant by restoring them when they cry out to him in repentance. By the end of Judges, God does not provide restoration or rest because the rebellion of the people is so great that no repentance comes.

During 1 and 2 Samuel, Israel's rejection of God's kingship and their desire to have a king (not just a judge) like the other nations (1 Sam 8:1-9) will bring God's judgment, but, even God's judgment will show his power and uniqueness. On one occasion God's judgment falls on Israel when the Ark of the Covenant falls into the hands of the Philistines. However, even this catastrophic event fails to create doubt about the fact that the God of Israel is the only God. Instead, it serves to remind us again that he is the sovereign king as he topples and then decapitates the statue of Dagon, the God of the Philistines, and as he brings tumors upon the Philistines themselves (1 Sam1-7). Even as God blesses the nation under the leadership of David and Solomon, we must never forget that Israel rejected the kingship of God in order to be like the other nations, Samuel's warnings about the danger of kings (1 Sam 8:4-18), and the debacle of Saul's reign. God chose Israel to be a kingdom of priests and tasked them with bringing his blessing to the nations rather than being like them, the decision to have a king foreshadows judgment from God.

In 2 Samuel 7, God has given David (and the people) rest from their enemies. David then desires to build a Temple for the worship of God in the place where God has chosen to put his name (Deut 12:1-28). After initially receiving a positive word from Nathan about doing so, God reveals to the prophet that David will not build him a place to dwell, but in this denial of David's desire, God displays his greatness, faithfulness, and eternality. He promises to make David's name great (compare with Genesis 12:1-3), and rather than David building God a house, God will build

David a house (a kingdom) and a throne that will endure forever. So, just as the God made promises to Abraham, he now makes further promises to David.

Before David died, God chose Solomon over Adonijah to be the king because God's gracious choice, not birth order, continues to establish who will carry on God's plan to bring his blessing to the nations. Solomon recognizes that his kingship fulfills God's promise to place one of David's sons on the throne, and his reign gets off to an excellent start. In response to God's command, Solomon asks for wisdom from God and receives this blessing, along with wealth an honor, but he rebels against God by making an alliance with the Egyptian Pharaoh by marrying his daughter (2 Kings 3:1-2; See Exod 34:10-28). This decision foreshadows even greater rebellion against the commands of God in the days to come.

When Solomon completes the Temple, we should recognize once again that God is near his people yet separated from them by the veils that guard the entrance to the Inner Sanctuary. After the priests placed the Ark of the Covenant into the Inner Sanctuary, the glory of God descended into the sanctuary in a cloud so thick that the priests could not stand to minister (1 Kings 8:10-11; 2 Chron 5:2-14). The writer of Chronicles explains that following Solomon's prayer to dedicate the Temple fire came down from heaven, consumed the burnt offerings and sacrifices, and again the glory of the Lord filled the

Temple. Notice the type of worship that this display of the amazing power of God provokes in his people. They worship and give thanks to God for his goodness because "his steadfast love endures forever" (2 Chron 7:1-3).

Take note of three important things that the dedication of this house tells us about God. First, when God displays his glory, his people experience this revelation as goodness and love (Exod 33:12-34:9). Second, even though this building symbolizes the intersection of heaven and earth where God reigned among his people, Solomon acknowledges before God and declares to the people that God is too great for heaven and the highest heaven to contain, so no one should believe that God could be contained in this building. Third, we must remember that God's glory can display his goodness and love even as he judges his people. Solomon's prayer makes it clear that the people will fail and deserve God's wrath, but he calls upon the God who brought them up out of Egypt to redeem them because they are his chosen people.

God Judges His People

Moses exhorted the children of Israel to have undivided loyalty to God as they entered into the Promised Land. From that time forward, God's ejection of Israel from the Land and into an extended exile had been inevitable. God's holiness will demand a just punishment for his people even though his faithfulness guarantees their redemption. In Deuteronomy 30:1-6, Moses declares that the curse of exile will come upon Israel for her rebellion but also promises that God will gather people from all the places where he has scattered them and will change their hearts so that they can love him. As we have just seen, Solomon's dedication of the Temple reiterated Moses' warning, but he called upon God to forgive and restore them because he is faithful even when his people are not.

After Solomon died, the Northern and Southern Kingdoms that David had united are split in fulfillment of the judgment that God declared upon Solomon for his rebellion and idolatry (1 Kings 11:1-13). Throughout the rest of 1 and 2 Kings, the author concludes his account of each king's reign with the assessment of whether he did good or evil in the sight of the Lord and whether or not he led the people to worship idols.[26] Even when good kings arose, the people were still worshiping in unauthorized places (not the Temple) and were worshiping unauthorized gods.[27] God alone would be a king they needed. God alone would lead them to carry out their mission of conveying His blessing to the nations. Through the recounting of this history, we see that God's judgment of his people came after an exceedingly long period of time. God pursued his people with grace, loving-kindness, and longsuffering. However, God, in his holiness, would not allow his covenant people to worship idols and to rob him glory that he deserved forever. Eventually, God will employ the pagan nations to send Israel into exile.

Before transitioning to the next stage of God's plan, don't forget that, while the kings were leading the people into rampant idolatry, God was raising up prophets to declare the truth to his people. These preachers warned both the Northern and Southern Kingdoms that they must turn away from idolatry or face banishment from the Land that God had graciously given them. Sadly, the people did not heed these warnings, and God used the Assyrians to destroy the Northern Kingdom and the Babylonians to destroy the Southern Kingdom. What the prophets declared would happen in the near future occurred according to the command of the Lord. Perhaps the most striking element of this judgment came from Ezekiel's vision of the glory of God departing from the Temple (Ezek 10). This departure of God's glory from the Temple symbolized the fact that judgment was about to take place.

Also, remember that the prophets' words of doom contained words of hope. After the coming destruction, God was going to redeem his people and cause all the nations to worship him. Throughout the entirety of Isaiah, the prophet declares that God will restore his people through the arrival of the Messianic Servant King who would signal that God was saving his people and forgiving their sin. This Servant King would bear the sin of God's people, would lead the people righteously, and would be a light to the nations. His rule would lead people from all nations to worship the one, true, and living God (Isa 42:1-9; 49:1-7; 60:1-22; 62:1-12). While Jeremiah presents some of the most startling descriptions of the coming destruction God is bringing, he also declares that God's intervention to restore his people after the Exile will be so magnificent that no one will ever talk about the Exodus deliverance ever again (Jer 16:14-15). Finally, Ezekiel declares that God will save his people not for their sake but for the sake of his own name (Ezek 36:22-32). The idolatry of his people has defiled the Land God gave them and has caused God's name to be mocked among the nations. So, God promises that he will vindicate the holiness of his own name by gathering his people from the nations where he scattered them to show off his sovereign power. He will cleanse them from their uncleanness to demonstrate his forgiveness. He will change their hearts and give them his Spirit to cause them to walk in his ways. Then, he will bless them with the fruitfulness of the Land to show that he is faithful to his promises.

As 2 Chronicles comes to a close, the Chronicler explains that God causes Cyrus to send the Israelites who want to return home back so that they can build a temple for Yahweh, the God of heaven. In Cyrus' declaration, God shows himself to be the sovereign ruler over all creation, who is also faithful to his promises, but the return doesn't make anyone forget the Exodus. Haggai and Zechariah declare that the rebuilt Temple doesn't yet have the same glory as Solomon's. In fact, Haggai rhetorically asks if this building is nothing when compared to the glorious Temple that God destroyed. While this declaration might seem harsh, he also encourages the people that God is with them and will soon act to reveal a greater glory in this Temple than the one built by Solomon had ever possessed (Hag 2:1-9). What then is the problem?

With the passing of years, the situation in Jerusalem grows dire because the wall around the city is in ruin. Upon hearing this news, Nehemiah begs God to intervene. God grants Nehemiah's prayer of repentance and request (Neh 1:4-11) and uses Artaxerxes, King of Persia, to send Nehemiah to Jerusalem to lead the already returned exiles in the rebuilding of the city wall (Neh 6:15-7:4). Yet, even with a rebuilt Temple, a rebuilt wall, and returned exiles, Nehemiah declares, through a recounting of Israel's history, what the problem is. Their sins have not been forgiven, and they still need God to forgive and redeem them (Neh 9:1-38).

The Old Testament story ends with Malachi's exhortation that the people must repent and prepare for the great day when God will return to his people. Malachi concludes by declaring that one like Elijah would prepare the way for the coming of the Lord by calling them to repent so that his arrival would be a joyous day in which God would dwell with his people rather than judge them (Mal 4:5-6).

This quick summary of the period after some Jews returned from Babylon demonstrates that those who were living in the midst of this unfolding story did not see themselves as living in the age where God's promises had been fulfilled. What is God going to do? When is God going to return to his people? While these questions seem to hover over the entirety of the Old Testament, two things should be clear. First, God is the main focus of the Scriptures. You are not the point of the Bible. God is. Before we understand what the Bible says about man (Arrow 4), we must observe what it tells us about God (Arrow 3). Second, you will notice that the attributes of God are consistent throughout the Scriptures. While different passages demonstrate various aspects of God's character, his person and work remains the same.

Every time you read the Bible imagine that you are turning a magnificent gem, with each turn revealing distinctive reflections of the glory of God. As our brief survey demonstrates, the Old Testament authors describe God as kind, loving, just, gracious, glorious, steadfast, forgiving, holy, and sovereign, along with many other similar attributes. When aiming at the target in Arrow 3, circle words that are used to describe God's character, or write them in the margin of your Bible or a journal. Using this technique will remind you of the character of God that is on display in the passage.

THE KING'S RETURN

Do you remember the opening pages of the story where God first presents his gracious plan to crush Satan, sin, and death and to overcome the brokenness that sin had created in his people and in his creation? Do you remember the promises that God made to Abraham and to David? Jesus completes God's plan and his promises. As a result, we should recognize that the Old Testament repeatedly points us forward to a king who is different from all the rest and will redeem his people. In the New Testament, the authors will describe Jesus' life and reflect upon what he accomplished in his death and resurrection by making specific references to theological themes and imagery from the Old Testament. When we recognize these references, we will be stunned by the unity of the Bible's narrative from Genesis to Revelation. So, when we have aimed Arrows 1 and 2 correctly, we will be prepared to see what the original authors were teaching their audiences and how that message then fits into God's plan.

John's description of the Word becoming flesh and Matthew's account of the birth of Jesus are great examples on the interconnectedness of Jesus' story with the story of God in the Old Testament.

God Dwells with His People in the Coming of His Son

In John 1:1-18, John the Apostle proclaims to his readers that Jesus of Nazareth was and is God in the flesh through his description of Jesus as the personified living, powerful, and active Word of God. By using this metaphor from the Old Testament to describe Jesus, John is declaring that Jesus the Messiah is the ultimate revelation of who God is and what saving activity looks like.[28]

In these verses, we recognize that John, writing after the resurrection, knew Jesus was both the Messiah (king) and God in the flesh. To demonstrate this claim, John draws on the language of the creation story to assert that the Word was eternal and equal with God and possessed every quality that defines God the Father as God. He also painstakingly differentiates the Word from the rest of creation. Everything else in the universe *was created*, but the Word *was*. The Word was God, was in intimate fellowship with God, and was the one through whom everything was created (John 1:1-5). In 1:9, John asserts, "The true light, which shines on every person, was coming into the world." The true light overcomes the darkness (a symbol of sin, confusion, and opposition to God's purposes in the gospel) and gives the right to become children of

God to all who believe (John 1:12).

In 1:14, John provides a stunning picture of how God the Son invaded the world as the eternal Word, became flesh, and pitched his tent among his people. This language of "pitching his tent" among the people would have evoked images of God dwelling in the Tabernacle as his people wandered in the wilderness and then as he conquered the Promised Land. Even though God was close to his people in the Old Testament, the tent of meeting was outside the camp, and God dwelt behind the veil of the Tabernacle. John explains that when people saw the face of Jesus, they were seeing the glory of the one and only from the Father, who was full of grace and truth.[29] Finally, John declares that the grace, which was given in the Law, has been replaced with a superior kind of grace and truth that comes through Jesus the Messiah, who perfectly makes God the Father known (John 1:17-18).[30]

In Matthew's birth narrative, Matthew describes how the Magi came from the east to worship Jesus as the new Jewish King. This news excites Herod's paranoia that and causes him to embark upon a plan to exterminate this potential rival by killing all of the children in Bethlehem under the age of two. Matthew explains the fleeing of Jesus' family to Egypt and the murdering of the children in and around Bethlehem by citing two texts from the Old Testament and asserts that these events fulfill the word spoken by the prophet. The first citation comes from Hosea 11:1, where Hosea's recounts Yahweh's use of the history of Israel in his legal accusation against the Northern Kingdom. These indictments show that God is just in destroying the kingdom. Matthew then draws out the implications of this original passage to create a comparison between Israel's failure and the true and faithful Israelite, Jesus. So, in the same way that Israel came up out of Egypt in the Exodus, Jesus the Messianic King will also take that journey and establish a new Exodus. [31]

The second quotation, from Jeremiah 31:15, reveals that this horrific slaughter is the fulfillment of God's plan. In the original passage, the prophet explains that Rachel is weeping because the descendants of her son Benjamin have been destroyed by God's judgment, but in the next verse God makes the exhortation to cease weeping because he will restore them and give them the hope of a new covenant. God then promises to write this covenant on their hearts so that they, from the least to the greatest, will know the Lord (Jer 31:1-40). So, Matthew employs this reference to Jeremiah 31:15 to describe the mourning that would have taken place in and around Bethlehem and to assert that Jesus, God's True King, has come and will be everything that Herod was not. This King will bring an end to the misery of God's people, will complete God's promise to forgive their sins (Matt 1:20-21), and will establish God's eternal kingdom. Ultimately, Matthew is saying that your mourning is about to turn into dancing (Jer 31:13)![32]

God Re-Establishes His People in the Life of His Son

As Jesus' ministry begins, Matthew again demonstrates the faithfulness of God to his promises as John the Baptist fulfills his task of preparing the way for the arrival of the King like Malachi prophesied. John prepares for the coming kingdom by calling them to repent. Jesus' ministry establishes the God's reign and fulfills the prophecy from Isaiah 40 that a voice would cry out from the wilderness preparing the way for God's return to his people.

As John baptizes people because they repented, he also has a word of warning about the judgment that soon awaits the religious leadership in Jerusalem. He explains that their lives must show the fruit that comes from true repentance because one mightier than he is coming who will baptize his people with the Holy Spirit. The giving of the Holy Spirit was one of the promises that God made to act as a sign that the Exile was over, but those who reject God's Messiah would remain under God's wrath and separated from his presence. Even though John hesitates to baptize Jesus when he arrives on the scene, Jesus commands him to do so to fulfill all righteousness. While Jesus himself was not guilty of sin, his baptism symbolizes his people's need for repentance that will prepare them for the arrival of God's kingdom.[33]

Jesus' baptism stands as the foundational moment from which his ministry is launched. The heavens are ripped open, indicating the intervention of God in history; the Spirit descends upon Jesus; and God confirms that Jesus is his Son in whom he is well pleased. In this declaration about Jesus, God the Father fuses together the role of Israel's king (Ps 2:7) with the role of the Servant of Yahweh (Isa 42:1). Jesus will suffer on behalf of God's people by bearing their sins, will bring an end to the Exile, will reestablish God's Kingdom and God's people, and will reveal God's glory to the nations, but this reality should not surprise us because Matthew has been declaring from the first verse of his Gospel that Jesus is the *messianic king!*[34] Take note of how N. T. Wright, a world-renowned New Testament scholar, sums up what the baptism of Jesus teaches us about Jesus' vocation,

> *A royal figure? Yes, people believed that such a figure would rule, bring justice to the whole world, and smash the pagans with a rod of iron. The servant? Yes, the servant would suffer and die; the servant people would bear a heavy load, leading not least to martyrdom. And God himself? Israel's God would come back to dwell with his people; devout Jews believed it. That was why it was so important to rebuild or cleanse the Temple.*[35]

The baptism makes the earth-shattering claim that the roles of the Servant, Messiah, and God himself returning to his people have been fused together in one person, who will establish God's Kingdom through his suffering on the cross, not through the Temple.[36]

The final piece in Matthew's introduction to the person of Jesus the Messiah comes in his description of the Jesus' temptation. The striking similarities between this story and the story of the Exodus must not be missed. Notice how Jesus fasted in the wilderness for *forty days* and *forty nights*. Matthew emphasizes a corresponding amount of time (forty days vs. forty years) and the great block that caused the wilderness generation to accuse God of bringing them to the wilderness to die—an empty stomach. With the stage now set by the Holy Spirit, the tempter comes onto the scene and begins to question whether or not Jesus truly is the Son of God and finally tempts him with idolatry.[37]

"*If you are the Son of God…*" These two temptations from the devil focus on Jesus' identity as the Son of God and allude to the Exodus story, where Israel is described as God's firstborn son (Exod 4:21-23), and Jesus' baptism. In this passage, Matthew continues to depict Jesus as king standing in the place of his people. When the devil tempts Jesus to turn the stones to bread to prove that he is God's son, Jesus quotes Deuteronomy 8:3 where Moses explains to the people that God has brought them through these wanderings for forty years so that he could humble them and cause them to understand that they did not live from the bread that filled their stomachs but from all that God had revealed about himself. Jesus trusts that God will provide for his needs because God has completely revealed who he is to Jesus.[38] Satan then tempts Jesus to jump off of the Temple to prove that he is the Son of God. Jesus responds by quoting Deuteronomy 6:16 in which Moses exhorts the children of Israel not to doubt the faithfulness of their God like they did at Massah and Meribah (Exod 17 and Num 20), where they accused him of breaking the covenant because they were thirsty. Jesus demonstrates trust in God that frees him from concerns about his identity as the Son of God.[39]

Finally, when tempted to be an idol worshiper, Jesus quotes Deuteronomy 6:13. In its original context, this exhortation to fear and serve God alone follows a reminder of the great deliverance from Egypt that God had performed and precedes the exhortation to reject other gods because God is a jealous God and they are his special people. If they insist on provoking the jealousy of God by following idols, they can be assured that judgment will come. Later, Moses will describe this judgment as ejection from the Land and a return to slavery. Jesus, the true Son of God remains faithful to the Father and triumphs over the devil unlike so many of the kings who came before him.[40]

Jesus passes this test in every way where Israel as

a nation failed in every perceivable way. In the rest of Matthew's Gospel, we will recognize that Jesus, the Son of God, is the true Israelite and is the Son of Abraham (Matt 1:1) through whom God accomplishes his purpose of blessing the nations and in whom he enacts his return to Zion (the Temple).[41]

God Redeems His People in the Death and Resurrection of His Son

In Matthew 21, Jesus enters Jerusalem on a colt, the foal of a donkey. Jesus has intentionally fulfilled Zechariah 9:9. This passage describes the entry of the messianic king, who brings with him righteousness and salvation to his people. Matthew's description of these events demonstrates that Jesus offers himself to Israel as her king in an explicit fashion. Jesus offers himself, however, as a king of peace not as a king of war in keeping with the prophetic word of Zechariah not with the popular expectation that the Messiah would establish God's kingdom through a military victory. We should also notice another element of Zechariah's prophecy. He also proclaims that this event will signify the return of God to his people and the end of their exile. So, in his entry into Jerusalem, Jesus is offering himself to Israel as her king and declaring that God has returned to Zion[42] Yet, when he enters the Temple both as the King who has authority over the Temple and as God returning to his people (2 Sam 7:12-14; Zech 6:9-14), no one recognizes his arrival because the Temple leadership has set itself against the purposes of God.[43]

As the final week of Jesus' life progresses, his conflict with the religious leaders will intensify. In Mark's Gospel, the cursing of the fig tree surrounds the action of Jesus in the Temple (Mark 11:12-25) and foreshadows the destruction that Jesus will prophesy in Mark 13. The Temple, which was meant to *symbolize* the intersection of heaven and earth, has been replaced by Jesus the Messiah, who *is* the intersection of heaven and earth (John 1:14).[44] The Temple and its leadership are under God's wrath, still in exile, because they have rejected God's Messiah who has come to bring God's forgiveness.

The great irony of the final week of Jesus' life is that the religious leaders, who plot to kill Jesus, are being used by God the Father to accomplish the task that he has ordained for the Son to complete. The religious leaders were the human causes of the death of Jesus, but no power on earth could have put Jesus on the cross apart from the will of God and the will of Jesus (John 10:18)! God the Father sends Jesus to the cross as the Suffering Messiah in order to establish his kingdom, enact judgment on sin, and redeem his people.

Jesus' sacrificial death establishes a new covenant through the shedding of his blood (Mark 14:22-25; Matt

26:26-29; Luke 22:14-23) and makes the forgiveness of sins (Matt 26:28), one of the promises associated with the end of the Exile (Isa 27:2-11, 40:1-2, 43:1-44:28, 52:13-54:17, 59:1-21; Jer 31:34; 33:8), possible. The death and resurrection of Jesus stands as the turning point of the Bible's story. These twin events complete the promises that God made to Abraham, establish God's eternal kingdom, and accomplish God's triumph over the ultimate enemies of his people–sin and death.[45] All people who repent and believe in King Jesus will be forgiven of their sins, will have a new identity in Christ (Gal 3:14; 2 Cor 5:16-21), and will be adopted into God's family (Gal 4:1-7).

This portion of the Bible's story transforms our understanding of God. First, Jesus, the Word made flesh, possesses all of the attributes that make God the Father God (John 1:1-3), yet Paul would still affirm that there is only one God (1 Cor 8:6). Second, Jesus' establishment of God's Kingdom demonstrates that the triune God is the *Sovereign King of the universe*. Third, God's *holiness* is on full display in that he remains untouched by sin, as God the Son lives among unholy people and remains untouched and unstained by their sin. Additionally, God acts *righteously* as he pours out his wrath against sin on Messiah Jesus, who bears the weight of sin, in the place of his people so that he can be *just* in the way he punishes sin and show his *saving power* to those who believe in Jesus (Rom 3:21-26). This action of God to *redeem* his people demonstrates once again that he is *faithful* to his promises even when his people are rebellious (Gal 3:6-14). Finally, the sending of the Son into the world reminds us that God demonstrates his *love* for the world by sending his Son into the world so that whoever believes in him would not perish but have everlasting life (John 3:16-17).[46]

THE KING'S REIGN

In the resolution of our story, God fulfills his promise to bring his blessing to the nations through the church, the true Israel.[47] Even though these people whom Jesus has redeemed still struggle with sin, the Spirit dwells in them and empowers them to live in obedience to Jesus' command to make disciples of all nations (Acts 1:8; 2 Cor 5:11-21). To demonstrate how God works to bring his blessing to the nations, we will examine the work of the Spirit to embolden the followers of Jesus to conquer the world with the gospel in Acts. Then, we will investigate the results of God's work to establish his people in Revelation 7 and Revelation 22.

The King Conquers the World

Luke weaves two central themes about the continuing work of God the Father and God the Holy Spirit throughout the course of Acts. First, God the Father is *sovereignly* and *providentially* carrying the message about his reign to the ends of the earth through the church. Polhill asserts, "That the mission of the church is under the direct control of God is perhaps the strongest theme in the theology of Acts."[48] God shows his power over the governmental and religious authorities as their actions often serve as catalysts for extending his kingdom and confirming the gospel.[49] Luke weaves the second theme together with the first as he explains that God the Father expands the mission through the indwelling power of the Holy Spirit who leads the church to carry the gospel to new frontiers, does the work of transforming sinners, and gives boldness to proclaimers of the good news.[50]

Luke begins the book of Acts with an opening word to connect his present work with the Gospel that he wrote previously. He explains that Jesus appeared to his disciples for forty days to confirm that he had conquered death. During this time, he teaches them about the arrival of God's Kingdom, which would be embodied by the redeemed people of God, the church and also orders them to remain in Jerusalem and wait for the Spirit whom the Father had promised.[51]

As Jesus is about to depart, Luke highlights the disciples' struggle to grasp the scope and to some degree the nature of what Jesus the Messiah will accomplish through his people when they ask if he is going to restore the kingdom to Israel at that time. Jesus responds that God's Kingdom will come on the earth but that they don't need to know when. In Acts 1:8, Jesus goes on to assert that they will receive power when the Holy Spirit comes to dwell in them and that they will be his witnesses in Jerusalem, Judea, Samaria, and to the ends of the Earth. This statement about the empowerment that will comes from the Holy Spirit, the task that they will have as witnesses, and the locations where this Spirit-empowered service will take place will serve as the topic sentence for the rest of the book.

In the paragraphs that follow, Luke shows how the disciples prepared for the coming of the Spirit. They recognized that Jesus had chosen twelve disciples, mirroring Jacob's twelve sons, to symbolize that these men would play a pivotal role in the launching of the true Israel. They replaced Judas with Matthias, someone who had been with them from the time of Jesus' baptism by John the Baptist and had seen the resurrected Jesus. With this symbolic number restored, they wait.

In Acts 2, Luke records how God filled Jesus' followers with the Holy Spirit. Notice that this event took place at the Feast of Pentecost, which first-century Jews associated with the giving of the Law at Sinai. This timing demonstrated that the people of God were now empowered directly by the Spirit of God in them rather than the Law that had no power to change them. To signify the arrival of the Spirit God provides the audible sign of a sound like a mighty, rushing wind and the visible sign of the tongues like flames of fire over their heads. When the crowd arrives to investigate this sound, the Spirit enables these believers to declare the message about Jesus with a boldness they had never before possessed, and they describe to the crowd the mighty works of God and proclaim these truths in the native languages of these Jews who have come to Jerusalem from the ends of the earth (Acts 2:1-13).

Peter then takes this opportunity to explain these events to the crowd. He declares that God has acted to fulfill the promise that he had made through Joel that in the last days God would pour out his Spirit on his people and that death and resurrection of Jesus of Nazareth, which established that he was both Lord and Messiah, makes this outpouring of the Spirit possible (Acts 2:14-36). He then exhorts them to repent and be baptized under the authority of Jesus who made this forgiveness of sins available.

Through the sending of the Spirit, God launches the church and empowers the members of this group for the mission to the nations. The result of Peter's preaching was that three thousand people were added to their number through repentance and faith in Jesus Christ. In Acts 2:42-47, Luke will summarize the characteristics of daily life in the early church. They were consistently learning from the apostles' teaching about Jesus, were gathering together in a community, and were going to the Temple to praise God for the work that he had done through Jesus. Luke illustrates the bond that Jesus' followers had as he describes their willingness to sell their possessions to meet the needs of those who were a part of church. God blessed this mission, and many more became followers of Jesus Christ.

As the narrative of Acts continues, Jesus continues to empower his people through the work of the Spirit. They are proclaiming the message about Jesus, and Jesus confirms the truthfulness of their preaching by visible demonstrations of his power that prove he has been raised from the dead. Their bold proclamation about God vindicating Jesus and establishing as Lord and Messiah infuriates the religious leaders and causes them to threaten the followers of Jesus (Acts 4:18-19; 5:27-42). Rather than cowering in fear, the church gathers and begs God to give them boldness to continue preaching while God confirmed their words by demonstrations of his power. Immediately, their request is granted (Acts 4:23-31).

God also acts to send his followers out of Jerusalem through the martyrdom of Stephen. As the narrative unfolds, the prayer for the boldness continues to be answered as the Holy Spirit speaks through Stephen in the synagogue. Because Stephen's opponents could not defeat him in a debate about Jesus, they instigate men to accuse Stephen of speaking against the Law and against God. Luke explains that Stephen had the face of an angel when he stood before the Sanhedrin to underline that he is speaking the very words of God and to take a shot at the Sadducees, who did not believe in angels. Stephen's central claims about God in the speech are that he has been faithful to a stubborn and idolatrous people, who have now made the Temple an idol, and has shown that faithfulness in an ultimate way through the sending of Jesus, whom they killed! In response to this sermon, the crowd attacks Stephen. Luke contrasts their rage with Stephen's calm. Stephen was full of the Holy Spirit, gazed into heaven, saw the glory of God, and is vindicated by Jesus who is standing at the right hand of God (Acts 7:2-8:1a). Even as they kill Stephen after a trial that mirrors the trial of Jesus, God accomplishing his purpose by using persecution to send the church on mission (Acts 8:1b).

God displays his sovereign power to accomplish his purposes once more when he conquers Saul the Pharisee, the greatest persecutor of the church (Acts 8:2-3), and employs him for carrying the gospel to the nations. The risen Jesus appears to Saul in his resurrected glory and knocks him down. In this encounter, Luke gives his readers a glimpse of the unity that exists between Jesus and his church. To persecute the church is to attack God the Son himself. Jesus then saves Saul and commissions him to declare Jesus' name to the Gentiles, kings, and the people of Israel and to suffer for the sake of his name (Acts 9:15-16). Immediately after having his sight restored and being filled with the Holy Spirit, Saul, whom we will come to know as Paul during his mission work among Gentiles, begins to do what he has been chosen and empowered to do (Acts 9:22-25). In the rest of Acts, Paul will declare the name of Jesus throughout the world and will establish a church everywhere that God saves people. Luke concludes Acts with Paul in Rome under house arrest and awaiting a trial before Caesar. While this situation might seem dire, Luke underscores the fact that in the heart of the empire (where Caesar was worshiped as a god and king) Paul has the opportunity to proclaim that the one, true God's reign has come in the death and resurrection of Jesus and that this Jesus is God and King (Acts 28:30-31).

The King Completes His Reign

While many theories exist concerning what Revelation describes about the return of Jesus, everyone should agree that John's central purpose in writing was to encourage the churches in Asia (and the churches that would come after them) that the Trinitarian God was sovereignly at work in history to remove Satan, sin, and death from his creation and to claim for himself a people from all the nations. Revelation also celebrates the One who sits on the throne and the Lamb and calls all of creation to worship. Finally, John presents the completing of God's eternal plan so that the people of God will reign over God's creation and will live forever in God's presence as he created them to do.

John constructs a vivid picture of each member of the Trinity as the drama of the book unfolds even as he exhibits great hesitancy in giving any physical description of what he saw around the throne of God to protect his readers from any temptation toward idolatry.[52] In Revelation 4, John describes everything around the throne in order to emphasize the great life-giving power (symbolized by the emerald rainbow), majesty, and inapproachability of the one who sits on that throne, but he does not describe the one the throne (Rev 4:5-6). John describes the throne of God in seventeen of Revelation's twenty-two chapters to emphasize that all other thrones, including Satan's and Caesar's, come under God's authority. John employs specific titles, like "the one who is, was, and is coming," "the first and the last," and "Alpha and Omega," to highlight the eternality of God over against the pagan gods who were created.[53] Finally, God rules over all creation because he made it all again in contrast with the pagan gods who did not create anything and only rule over certain parts of the creation. Consequently, the God *can* and *will* remake everything when he finally eradicates the enemies of God's people.[54]

John also explains that the risen Jesus is God in every way. He rules and is worshiped alongside God the Father. In chapter one, John describes his vision of Son of Man in language that echoes both the description of the Ancient of Days in Daniel 7 and the one like the children of men in Daniel 10 to demonstrate that Jesus is God in every way. When the Son of Man commands John to write, he explains to John that he had died and been raised from the dead and as such has the power over death and Hades. On other occasions, John will describe King Jesus as the "firstborn from out of the dead ones" and as the Lamb to emphasize that he has already conquered the ultimate enemies of God's people—sin and death—and guaranteed their final ruin. Finally, Jesus has the authority to approach the throne and take the scroll from God because he is equal with God and because he died as a sacrifice in the place of his people and ransomed them to complete God's promises of a worldwide family with a worldwide reign and a worldwide mission (Rev 5:9-11).[55]

Next, John describes God the Holy Spirit throughout the book as the divine spirit (seven spirits of God) who delivers this message. Additionally, John describes three occasions where he was carried away in the Spirit to receive the prophetic message from God. The Spirit is also at work to send a message from God through John directly to specific churches themselves (Rev 2:7, 11, 17, 29;

3:1, 6, 13, 22). Finally, the Spirit and the church work to call people to believe the message that brings salvation and eternal life (Rev 22:17).

John's depiction of how the story concludes focuses us on the fact that God deserves worship for who he *is* and what he *has done*. In Revelation 4-5, the worship of the One who sits on the throne emphasizes that God is *holy* (set apart from the sin of creation), *eternal*, *creator*, *sustainer*, and *worthy of glory*, and the worshipers proclaim that the Lamb is *worthy* because he was slain and ransomed God's people out of all the nations and has made them a kingdom and priests (echoing Exod 19:6) who will reign on the earth.[56] Throughout Revelation 14-15, John utilizes imagery that should remind us of the glorious ransoming of God's people in the Exodus. Notice the song of praise that the saints sing to God because of the work of the Lamb (Rev 15:2-4). They exalt God for his deeds, his *might*, his *justice*, his *kingship*, his *holiness*, his *righteous judgment*, and his *saving work*. All of these attributes and actions of God, even the undiluted wrath that is about to be poured out in Revelation 14, deserve praise! In chapter 19, a great multitude in heaven worships God. The multitude praises God for the *salvation*, *power*, and *glory* that belong to him and for the eternal *judgment* of those who have rejected his rule.[57] We must realize, however, that the saints do not rejoice because sinners are condemned. They rejoice because God's justice and their suffering is vindicated.[58]

Finally, God is praised because he has now brought about his perfect reign and is united with his bride.

The final piece to our puzzle is the conclusion of John's description of the New Jerusalem that comes down out of heaven from God through which he shows the nearness that nearness of God to his people in the new creation. John explains that the angel shows him the river of the water of life, which flows from the throne of God and the Lamb. Take note of the difference between the descriptions of the sea of glass that separates creation from the throne of God (Rev 4) and the river of the water of life, which describes the life-giving power that comes to God's people from his throne. John also explains that God's people have access to the tree of life because God has removed evil from his creation, his perfect reign has come, his people have been redeemed, and healing has come to the nations. The most striking element of John's account comes next. He explains that God's people will worship him and will see his face! Due to the fact that the Lamb has redeemed God's people and God has resurrected them, this purified and righteous people can see God's face (dwell in his presence) and have no fear. The people of God bear his mark and know him as they are known (Rev 22:1-6).

CONCLUSION

Well, you made it to the end! You might be wondering why this chapter is so much longer than all of the rest. The answer is simple. God is the main character in the Bible. Think about how many television shows are named after the main character. Seinfeld, which was reportedly about "nothing," was actually about Jerry and how he interacted with the strange crew that revolved around him. Other characters like Elaine, George, Kramer, NEWMAN!, and Frank might appear in a scene, but they are not the center of the story. You could have the show without any of these other characters, but you cannot have the show without Jerry. The same thing is true of the Bible. God shows up on every page, even when no one uses his covenant name, like in the book of Esther. Other characters come and go, but they only come onto the stage for the purpose of helping us understand better who God is and what he is accomplishing.

Think about the main point of some classic Bible stories. The story of David and Goliath is not a story about conquering the giants in your life but is a story about God's sovereign power over the pagans and their gods. When Jesus healed the paralytic in Mark 2:1-12, Mark is not teaching about the importance of bringing your friends to Jesus. He is demonstrating through the healing miracle that Jesus is the Messiah, Son of God, has authority from God to forgive sins. The story about Jesus feeding the five thousand is not encouraging us to share like the little boy who shared his lunch. John uses the story to reveal that Jesus is the Messiah, Son of God so that his readers would believe in him.

Your task is first to read every story to determine what the passage says and what it meant to its original audience. If your answers to those questions do not include something about the triune God, you probably need to aim again. I have poor vision without corrective lenses. If I tried to aim anything without my glasses or contacts, whoever is around me better watch out! If you read the Bible and fail to engage with the question asked in this Arrow, your aim will be off, and your reading of the Bible could hurt you or someone around you. That reason alone demands a lengthy chapter like this one!

As we conclude this God-centered journey through the Bible, several themes demand to be repeated. First, throughout the Scriptures, we learn that *God is one* (Deut 6:4) and that he reveals himself in *three persons*. Second, the triune God is the *Sovereign King of the universe* because he is the *creator*, and he deserves and demands undivided loyalty from the humans that he has made in his own image. Due to the failure of God's people to heed his commands, we begin to learn about the third fundamental fact. God is both *just* and *holy*. In his *holiness*, he is untouched by the effects of sin, and his *justice*, in keeping with his *holiness*, must be executed against the rebellion of humanity. So, God chooses Abraham to be the one through whom he (God himself) will set things right again in his creation. In choosing Abraham and his family, *God establishes a covenantal relationship* that is entirely dependent up him to fulfill (Gen 15) and shows his *providential* care as he continues to stand by his people even though they repeatedly rebelled against his rule. Next, we see that God is *faithful* to his promises as he sends his own Son to fulfill this promise of bringing the blessing of his presence to the nations and the forgiveness of sins to his own people and the world. Finally, due to all of God's attributes and actions, *he alone deserves the worship of his creatures.*

ARROW 4:
WHAT DOES THIS PASSAGE TELL US ABOUT MAN?

This Arrow shifts our focus from the central character in the Bible's story (God) to human beings. In making this shift, we must *not* fall into the trap of making the characters of the Bible stories the focus of the text or seeing them simply as examples to follow (or to avoid!). This misstep can take us away from the God-centered nature of the Bible and cause us to miss the work of God that was necessary for them to be used by him. Our exploration of the story of God reveled that he created people to bear his image, live in communion with him, worship him, and extend his rule throughout the creation. In this way, humans are distinct from the rest of God's creation, but the rebellion of Adam and Eve in the garden has affected both humanity and all of creation. Finally, the previous chapter showed how God intervened to restore not only humanity but also all of creation through the death and resurrection of Jesus.

Previously, we divided the story of the Bible into the following parts: *The King's Reign*, *The King's Judgment*, *The King's Return*, and *The King's Reign*. I (Donny) want to mirror those sections as we look at humanity's place in the Bible's story with the following sections: *Image Bearers*, *Rebels*, *the Redeemed*, and *Regents*. So, as we retrace our steps a bit and investigate the place of humanity in the story of God's work to recreate his people and his creation, pay particular attention to three things: how the creation story demonstrates that people are made in God's image, how the rest of the story demonstrates that they are sinners in rebellion against God, and how being recreated in Christ makes believers new creations and provides them with the freedom to flourish by serving King Jesus.

IMAGE BEARERS

In Genesis 1-2, God creates everything out of nothing and displays his reign over everything that he has made. At the end of the creation narrative in Genesis 1, God made one creature who was distinct from the rest. God created man and woman in his image and after his likeness and gave them the responsibility of governing all that he had made (Gen 1:26). God also blessed them; commanded them to be fruitful, multiply, and fill the earth; and gave them food to eat. God provided everything they needed to live in communion with him and to flourish forever.[59]

When the transition is made into Genesis 2, we learn the specifics of how God created both man and woman and the garden that God has provided for them to tend and enjoy. God creates man out of the dust of the ground and breathes life into him. God makes a garden as a dwelling place for him. It has trees that were pleasant to his sight and were good for food. God is meeting all of man's needs both for sustenance and enjoyment. God places the man in the garden to care for it, but this work is easy and joy-filled because God created him specifically for it. Along with all of this blessing and provision, God gave one prohibition. Genesis 2:16-17 states, "And the LORD God commanded the man, saying, 'You may surely eat of every tree of the garden, but of the tree of the knowledge of good and evil you shall not eat, for in the day that you eat of it you shall surely die.'"

Following this prohibition, we learn for the first time that things are not good because Adam did not have a helper fit for him. God again provides all that Adam needed for joy and flourishing by giving him woman. So, God created Adam and Eve in his image to care for his creation by doing what each were created to do. Since we live after the fall where work is difficult, we struggle to understand how Adam and Eve's perfect fellowship with God made this work a joy. What could be better than knowing God without being stained by sin and doing what he made you to do? Nothing.

What does it mean for Adam and Eve (and all humanity) to have been created in God's image?[60] As we consider the creation narrative and the Bible as whole, we should recognize that God was *not* meeting some kind of need by creating humanity. God created us for his own glory because he deserves the worship and the honor that people bring him as they fulfill his command to be fruitful, multiply, fill the earth, and to extend his wise rule throughout all of his creation.[61] So, our purpose is to live lives of worship, focused on displaying God's greatness, goodness, and glory for our great benefit, joy, and pleasure.[62] Wayne Grudem, a noted theologian and author, defines the creation of people in the image of God in the following way: "*The fact that man is in the image of God means that man is like God and represents God* [emphasis original]."[63] This statement explains that being made in the image of God is not primarily defined by what we do or our relationships with others but rather by who we *are*. Efforts to distill the image of God in man down to one single quality are pointless. Every quality that defines us as humans and distinguishes us from the rest of creation shows that God has made us and that we bear his image.[64] Additionally, no person bears more of the image of God than another.[65] Ponder then Grudem's assertion that

> As we read the rest of Scripture (beyond the
> creation account in Genesis), we realize that a
> full understanding of man's likeness to God would
> require a full understanding of who God is in his
> being and in his actions and a full understanding
> of who man is and what he does. The more we
> know about God and man the more similarities
> we will recognize, and the more fully we will
> understand what Scripture means when it says that
> man is made in the image of God. The expression
> refers to every way in which man is like God.[66]

Consider the order of the application questions in
Seven Arrows. They begin with God. When we begin to
grasp the qualities God possesses and gives to us, we see
glimpses of those same qualities in other humans (even
in our redeemed or unredeemed sinfulness) for we are
reflections of the God who made us. When the order gets
switched, we begin to create a God made in our image
rather than the God of the Bible.

For example, perhaps you are a young female
struggling with self-worth in a world where some
measure worth by how you look in comparison to an
air-brushed model on a magazine cover. Your need will
not be satisfied in a self-help manual or the latest health
craze but through the realization that God created you
and gave you a worth and value grounded in the worth

and value of your creator. Or, perhaps you're a retiree whose children have long since left your home, and you are struggling with loneliness and depression. Your worth will not be demonstrated in your ability to pick up another hobby to pass the time but in the realization that age has not diminished the image of God in you and that you have a vital role to play in God's mission in the world as long as he gives you life. Your church needs you! As Mrs. Linda Brown, a treasured friend of ours who has retired and faithfully serves The Church at Cherrydale, told my wife when Amber thanked her for coming and serving each day, "Well, I can only take so many naps." Knowing that God created you in his image and has work for you to do should inspire you to work and bring you joy in doing it (Col 3:22-25).

Now, we must face the question of how sin affects the fact that we are made in the image of God. What happened in the fall? What happened after the fall? And, why do these things matter?

REBELS

In Genesis 3, Adam and Eve rebel against God's reign and receive God's curse. Their sin fractures the perfect communion that they had with God and results in an attempt to hide from the presence of God. Even though they still bear God's image and still receive his care (see Gen 3:15, 21), their sinfulness separates them from him. The curses do not change the commands to work and care for God's creation and to be fruitful and multiply. The curses simply make accomplishing them hard and difficult. While work can still bring satisfaction, it also brings weariness. While the command to be fruitful and fill the earth still brings joy, the pain of childbirth is multiplied. While the one flesh relationship between a man and a woman still makes life *good*, they will both rebel against their God-ordained roles in it. This final curse reflects their desire to subvert God's leadership over them.[67] Along with Adam and Eve, the whole creation receives the curse as well because its rulers have rebelled against God. As a result, the ground will produce weeds rather than fruit, and the animals, rather than living in harmony with one another, will be at war. The ultimate curse, however, will be death (Gen 3:19).

Catastrophe and Chaos

As the story of Genesis unfolds, we see that the fall has affected all of the sons and daughters of Adam and Eve. Their sinfulness gives birth to all manner of rebellion against God. Cain becomes angry with God because his offering was not accepted and kills his brother whose offering was accepted. As the story of Cain's descendants continues, the evil multiplies (Gen 4:17-24). Once we reach Genesis 6:5, we see the extent of the sinfulness of humanity in the following summary statement: "The LORD saw that the wickedness of man was great in the earth, and that every intention of the thoughts of his heart was only evil continually." Throughout the rest of the Old Testament, this summary statement is the perfect description of humanity apart from the gracious work of God to make them his people.

So, as we read the Scriptures and ask *What does this passage say about man?*, we must consider what the passage reveals about the sinfulness of humanity apart from the grace of God. This reality will make Bible reading both joyous and painful. Around every turn we are going to be reminded of the glory and majesty of God *and* the depth of our sin. Facing this fact will help us to find our place in both the story of God and the story of man.

When these stories become our story, our identity can begin to be defined by who God is (God's story) and who he has made us to be in Christ (man's story). We can then begin to see that all of the competing stories from the world are fiction and will never satisfy. We can begin to know at the core of who we are that the Psalmist was correct when he said, "Because your [God's] steadfast love is better than life, my lips will praise you" (Ps 63:3).

God moves his story forward by destroying the wicked in the flood, but even in this act of judgment, he shows great grace by saving Noah and his family. The story of Noah, however, underlines the awfulness of human rebellion. God chose Noah and used him to continue the divine plan, but Noah and his children are still rebels. After the waters recede, God renews his command to be fruitful and multiply and fill the earth. He also explains that humans and animals will be adversaries from this point forward and, finally, pledges that he will not destroy the earth with a flood ever again. Immediately following this gracious encounter with God, Noah gets drunk and lays down naked in his tent. Ham sees the nakedness of his father and is cursed because of the sin. The stain of sin remains—even in those who belong to God.

Covenantal Hope

As we saw in the previous chapter, the story reaches another pivotal point when we come to Genesis 11. In this passage, humanity directly rebels against God's plan to be fruitful and multiply and fill the earth. So, God confuses their speech and disperses them. God then calls Abram and his family to be the ones he would use to bless all the families of the earth. However, even in Abram and Sarai's family, we can see the effect of the fall in their childlessness. Being fruitful is difficult. In spite of their childlessness, Abram believes God's promise, and God credited it to him as righteousness (Gen 15:6). In light of this faith in God's promise (and ultimately in God), God covenants with Abram to give the Promised Land to Abram's descendants after rescuing them from slavery in Egypt. The unprecedented nature of this covenant, culturally speaking, is that the responsibility for keeping the covenant falls on the master and not the servant.

All of the things that God promised to Abram came to pass. God gave him the promised son and grew his family. God saved his family from the famine by sending Joseph to Egypt ahead of them, and rather than departing when the famine was over, they became sojourners there (Gen 39-50). As God had foretold, they became slaves of the Egyptians and seemingly forgot their God even though he was still blessing them with children. Eventually their plight becomes so awful that they cry out to God, and in his grace he hears their cries and intervenes to free them and sends Moses to lead (Exod 1-4).

God enacts the plagues to demonstrate that he alone is God and that the Egyptian gods are not—especially the Pharaoh who believed he was a god. In the final plague, God kills all of the firstborn males belonging to Egyptian households but spares the Israelite children because of the blood that he commanded them to put on the doorposts of their homes (Exod 5-12). God then delivers them through the Red Sea by parting it, and he destroys Pharaoh's army by closing it on them. God continues to lead Israel to the Land that he was going to give them. The people, however, fail miserably in their attempts to follow and trust God, even after these great revelations of his might (Exod 13-14). Every time that their stomachs get empty or their mouths get dry, they accuse God of bringing them out in the wilderness to die, and eventually they even complain about the food that God has provided (Exod 16; Num 20-21).

At a pivotal moment in the journey, God calls Moses up to Mount Sinai. Since God chose them and has now delivered them, he commands the people to obey his voice, to live as a holy nation, which means *distinct* or *separate*, and to be a kingdom of priests who lead the nations to worship the one, true, and living God (Exod 19).[68] When the people see the evidences of God's presence on the mountain, they fear that hearing his voice again would cause them to die. So, they beg Moses to go and hear the words of God in their place (Exod 20:18-21). When Moses retells this story as they prepare to enter into the Promised Land, he explains that God said they were right in all that they said (Deut 5:28-29). This episode displays the heart of the problem. Israel is sinful just like every other nation and will not be obedient for long. Only God can bless the world.

When Moses goes up on the mountain to commune with God, the people begin to fear that Moses has died and decide to break the second commandment, at the least, by making a golden image to go before them. In response, God both punishes them and shows them grace (Exod 32-33). When they reach the borders of the Land that God has promised to give them, they doubt his power to give them victory and rebel against his kingship. So, they wander around in the wilderness until everyone of the Exodus generation, except for Joshua and Caleb, has died.

Just before his death, Moses gathers the people on the plains of Moab and prepares them for what lies ahead across the Jordan River by preaching to them about their past and warning them about the future. He sets before them the way of life and the way of death. The way of life is an invitation from God to commune with him in worship, as they love the Lord their God with all of their emotions, intellect, strength, and possessions. [69] At its core, the way of death is characterized by making idols and worshiping other gods. In Deuteronomy 27-30, Moses explains a ceremony in which the children of Israel will recite to one another the blessings that will come from obedience to God's law and the curses that will come from covenant infidelity. The final and ultimate curse would be ejection from the Land that God was about to give them. They would go into exile and return to slavery. Note what Moses says in the following quote from Deuteronomy 28:45-48:

> *All these curses shall come upon you and pursue*
> *you and overtake you till you are destroyed, because*

> *you did not obey the voice of the LORD your God,*
> *to keep his commandments and his statutes that*
> *he commanded you. They shall be a sign and a*
> *wonder against you and your offspring forever.*
> *Because you did not serve the LORD your God*
> *with joyfulness and gladness of heart, because of*
> *the abundance of all things, therefore you shall*
> *serve your enemies whom the LORD will send*
> *against you, in hunger and thirst, in nakedness,*
> *and lacking everything. And he will put a yoke of*
> *iron on your neck until he has destroyed you.*

Pay close attention to the fact that obedience to God and having abundant life in the Land was never going to come from checking off items on a list. Proper worship of God and obedience could only come from joyful and glad hearts that were celebrating continually the salvation that God had given when he led them out of Egypt and gave them the Promised Land. At this point, a problem arises. As the instruction in this sermon unfolds, the warnings get even worse and begin to sound more like a prediction than a simple warning. And, as we read through the rest of the Old Testament, we find that everything—all of the blessings and all of the curses—which Moses outlines comes to pass. In fact, these chapters are an outline for the historical books that will follow.

Covenantal Curse

In Joshua, God gives Israel the Land that he had promised to Father Abraham, who now had many sons ("And many sons had Father Abraham...so let's just praise the Lord!"). In Judges, we can discern where the story is headed as the people repeatedly fall into sin, receive the judgment of God by being under the rule of neighboring pagan kingdoms, repent from their rebellion, and receive restoration from God through the work of a judge. Eventually, God gives them a king, but their desire for a king should be a clue to us that Israel is in rebellion and is rejecting God's kingship. In the end, God sends all of Israel (both the Northern and the Southern Kingdoms) into exile because of its rebellion (Judg 1-21).

Why did this group of people rebel against God in such a profound way even after seeing the direct intervention of God to redeem them from slavery in Egypt and to give them the Promised Land? The simple answer is that they were filled with sin because they were sinners even before they were born. And, so are we. The rebellion of the children of Israel and our rebellion both go back to the Fall. Even though God, in his grace, gave his children these laws to provide a way for them to live in communion with him, they (like the pagans) inherited guilt and corruption from Adam and will continue as rebels apart from the transformation of the heart that God accomplishes.[70]

The fact that all people are by nature sinners does not mean that they practice unrestrained evil. God has given us governing authorities to punish evil, families and society to establish social conventions, and a conscience, but this sinful nature does infect every part of us.[71] As Grudem explains, "It is not just that some parts of us are sinful and others are pure. Rather, every part of our being is affected by sin—our intellects, our emotions and desires, our hearts (the center of our desires and decision-making processes), our goals and motives, and even our physical bodies."[72] So, as we consider what a passage says about man, we must consider sin's corrupting power in us and recognize sin as the enemy of our desire to know true flourishing. Sin offers us a promise of satisfaction apart from God's kingship and actually gives us emptiness.[73]

Sin (for now) is a part of who we are and affects what we do. We are all sinners, so we do sinful things. Perhaps you are reading the Bible and become convicted about a struggle you are having with an addiction. You hate the sin, but you just cannot stop doing it. Your temptation is to feel convicted for your actions, which you should, while forgetting the fact that these actions come from a sinful heart that is rebelling against God's kingship. The action is a symptom of a much deeper problem. If you are a Christian, your life is hidden with Christ in God (Col 3:3), which means that God's story *really* is your story. The only way that you can have freedom from that sin is for God's story to become so stunningly beautiful to you that the God who reveals himself in that story is the only one who can satisfy.

To conclude this part of man's story as it is lived out by Israel, we must realize that Israel was filled with people who were sinners just like the pagans. When God gave Israel the law, he was not giving them a way to earn favor with him so that they would become his people. They had received his favor. They were his people. The instructions that God gave them demonstrated God's gracious rule over Israel and their distinctiveness among the nations as his people. These instructions established a way for an unholy people to approach a holy God in worshipful living that would bring them immense satisfaction. Unfortunately, their sinful hearts caused them to despise God's wise rule and to think that they could meet their needs and find satisfaction by pursuing idols. This sin resulted in God's destruction of their nation. How then will God's promise be completed? Note what Moses says in Deuteronomy 30:1-6:

> And when all these things come upon you, the
> blessing and the curse, which I have set before
> you, and you call them to mind among all the
> nations where the LORD your God has driven you,
> and return to the LORD your God, you and your
> children, and obey his voice in all that I command
> you today, with all your heart and with all your
> soul, then the LORD your God will restore your

fortunes and have mercy on you, and he will gather
you again from all the peoples where the LORD
your God has scattered you. If your outcasts are
in the uttermost parts of heaven, from there the
LORD your God will gather you, and from there he
will take you. And the LORD your God will bring
you into the land that your fathers possessed, that
you may possess it. And he will make you more
prosperous and numerous than your fathers.
And the LORD your God will circumcise your
heart and the heart of your offspring, so that
you will love the LORD your God with all your
heart and with all your soul, that you may live.

The answer to the problem is God. He will act in grace to restore his people and change the hearts of his people so that they can love him with all of who they are and live in his presence forever. So, what is the result of the work of God to change the hearts of his people?

REDEEMED

The answer to humanity's problem is Jesus, the true human, the true Israelite, God in the flesh. In his life, Jesus models what living in perfect communion with God looks like. When tempted by the devil, he trusts in

God's provision. His longing for communion with the Father trumps any temptation (Heb 4:15). Throughout his ministry, Jesus communes with the Father in prayer (Mark 1:35-39; 6:45-47; 14:32-42; Luke 3:21; 5:16; 6:12; 9:18, 28-29; 11:1). No Gospel displays this communion more than John's in which Jesus claims to do only what he sees the Father doing. In John 5:19, after the healing of the lame man on the Sabbath, Jesus explains that this miracle of healing was in perfect harmony with the work of the Father (John 5:19-47). In John 7:15, Jesus explains that his teaching comes from the Father and has his authority (See also John 14:8-11). In John 10:22-30, Jesus teaches that the works he does in the Father's name bear witness about his identity and professes that he and the Father are one (See also John 8:48-59). In John 17, Jesus prays that God would unify his followers and those who would believe as a result of their witness so that the world would know that God sent Jesus and loves these believers as he loves Jesus. Finally, Jesus comes as the true Israelite king and bears the righteous judgment of God against sin, and in his resurrection defeats sin's coconspirator, death, so that believers can know God and live abundantly.

The person who has believed in and has been regenerated by Christ has become a new creation and has been united with Christ so that what is true of Christ is true of her even as she still struggles with sin. In 1 Corinthians 15 and Romans 5, Paul explains that humanity can only be divided into two groups, those who are restored in Christ and those who are in Adam. In 1 Corinthians 15, Paul asserts that those who are *in Adam* are oppressed by the power of sin and death and face God's judgment and that those who are *in Christ* have been freed from the power of sin and death and are long for their communion with God to be made complete in the resurrection from the dead (1 Cor 15:42-49). In Romans 5, Paul extols the fact that Christ died for the ungodly and makes the sinner right before God by faith in Christ so that they now can begin to live and flourish under the kingship of Jesus rather than the oppressive rule of sin and death. While these passages occur in different contexts in different letters, they share the common theme that you cannot live the soul-satisfying life—both now and into eternity for which you were made unless you belong to Jesus Christ, the resurrected King.

Paul also addresses this theme of the transforming work of God in saving those who trust Christ in 2 Corinthians 5:11-21. As Paul describes the ministry of reconciliation that Christ compels him to complete, he explains to the Corinthians that receiving life from Christ carries with it the responsibility of no longer living for themselves but living "for the one who died and was raised for them" (2 Cor 5:15). He then goes on to conclude that the one who is *in Christ*—that is *united* with him—is a new creation and because of this union with Christ he possesses the righteous status before God that Christ has. This new status provides Christians with the opportunity, even in this fallen world, to know God, love God, and live in fellowship with God—namely to experience what they were created for.

Let's summarize this part of the story. The redemption that Christ works in us allows him to change our story from an obituary to a birth announcement because he creates a new person who is a new creation.[74] We must remember, however, that redeeming and forgiving us are not the goal of God's work to save us. They make us fit for the blessing of communing with the God who has made us and brings true satisfaction.[75] In essence, God makes us truly human, recreated for our good and to grow in our knowledge of him. So, as we ask what the passage says about man, we must determine what (if anything) the passage says about who God has made us to be in Christ, who redeemed us from death, filled us with God's Spirit, and empowered us by God's Spirit to endure until our hope is realized in Christ's final victory (Rom 8).

AMBASSADORS

In this portion of the story, we transition from what Christ has made us to be into what he has called us to do through his church. The goal of obedience to Christ has much in common with what God commanded Adam and Eve to do in the garden and what he purposed for Israel to do in the Exodus.[76] In the New Testament letters, the authors will exhort believers to display *Kingdom Obedience* because Jesus Christ has transformed them and given them a place in his kingdom. This *Kingdom Obedience* then merges with God's purpose for his people to be a part of the *Kingdom Mission*. God's people obey so that they will shine as lights (Phil 2:15) in a sinful world and serve their King as his ambassadors, who declare that King Jesus has conquered the power of sin and death and offers resurrection life under his reign to all who will believe in him (2 Cor 5:18-20).

Kingdom Obedience

In all of his letters, Paul follows the portion of the message where he teaches the believers how their thinking must change with a section where he commands them to put this change of thinking into practice. Teaching the believers how to think was the best way to provide the foundation for how they were to live as Christ's ambassadors, have unity as a church, and make a kingdom difference in their communities. When we grow in the knowledge of who God is, we will then live our lives to display how the Holy Spirit has applied the truth that we have learned from the Scriptures. Paul's exhortations were not written as random items to check off of a to-do list so that God will love them more. Rather, Paul teaches them so that they will flourish in their fellowship with God. Disobeying these commands will injure both the one in sin and the church (1 Cor 5:1-8), and Paul wants to protect both. As you study the Scriptures, pay attention to how Paul connects a growing knowledge of who God is with obedience that brings glory to God.

Let's consider *Kingdom Obedience* further by considering how the love that Christ has for his church should cause his followers to love the church and then understand their need for biblical community in the church.

Christ's Love for His Bride

Has anyone ever told you that they love Jesus, but they did *not* want to have anything to do with the church? Or, has anyone ever told you that they can practice their kind of Christianity without the church? If someone said that to me, I would try to respond to this question in love and ask them to examine Ephesians 5:22-33 with me. This passage might seem like an odd choice because it occurs within a series of commands about how the various people in a Christian household are to relate to one another, but, if you look at the passage a little more closely, you will recognize that Paul is using the husband and wife relationship primarily as a metaphor to describe the love that Christ has for the church.

In Ephesians 5:22-24, Paul uses the leadership of the husband in the home to describe Christ's leadership of the church, which he describes as Christ's body. Since Christ is the head of the church, the church should submit to his kingship. That part seems simple enough, but how closely connected is your head to your body? If you are reading this book, I would guess that they are pretty close! Before we draw any conclusions, let's look at the next paragraph.

In Ephesians 5:25-33, Paul teaches his readers that Jesus Christ loved the church and died for the church, just as a man should love his wife and be willing to sacrifice his life for hers. Jesus died for the church with the purpose of setting her apart from the rest of sinful humanity having cleansed her with the teaching of Scripture, and he provides for his church, as a husband provides for his bride. Paul then concludes with the claim that God didn't just create marriage so that men and women could enjoy life together. Rather, God created marriage for these people who bear his image so that their love and concern for one another could be a reflection of the immense love that Christ has for his church.

How should a man respond if someone said to him, "I love you but cannot stand your wife?" He should say that is impossible since he and his bride are one. How would you respond to a spouse who says that his or her kind of marriage is one that does not require time spent together? I hope that you would confront that person with the fact that they do not seem to understand the nature of marriage at all. So, why do we think that Jesus could ever be pleased when someone tries to say something like that about his bride?[77] And, why do we think that we can grow in our *Kingdom Obedience* without the church?

Created for Community

I hope our examination of Ephesians 5:22-33 convinced you that loving Jesus means that you must love his bride and desire to live in community with other believers in the church. Because of our sinfulness, these relationships will be difficult, but in spite of that reality, Paul teaches we need each other so that someone who is consistently a part of our lives can confront us and restore us when we are tangled up in sin (Gal 6:1-5). We need people, who can encourage us when the pain of living in a world that is upside down because of sin becomes almost too difficult to bear (1 Thess 4:13-18, 5:12-22; 2 Cor 13:11). Let's examine two examples of Paul's exhortation to demonstrate love for God and one another through relationships in the church.

Paul's letter to the Galatian churches exemplifies how the apostle corrects theological errors before he corrects behavioral ones. Paul understood that their bad behavior was a symptom of the root problem of bad theology. So, if their thinking about what God had accomplished for them in Christ was corrected, their Spirit-enabled *kingdom obedience* would follow. In the body of the Galatian letter (1:6-4:31), Paul explains that submitting to the Law would actually result in a return to the slavery from which Christ had set them free rather than bring them closer to God as his opponents had claimed! He reinforced this fact by reminding them they began this journey with Christ by the Spirit and that they would finish it in the same way (Gal 3:1-5). Now that he has corrected their improper thinking about what Christ accomplished in his death, Paul applies this proper thinking to everyday living.

They have been freed from slavery (Gal 5:1), but this freedom from slavery to the law should not be an opportunity for sinful behavior (Gal 5:13a). Rather, this work of God should free them to demonstrate their love for God and one another through Spirit-empowered service not through obeying the Mosaic Law (Gal 5:13b-15). The one who walks in the Spirit will by definition not gratify the desires of the flesh from which the law tried unsuccessfully to protect Israel (Gal 5:16). In the end, as we have already seen, this love for one another will cause believers to do the messy work of walking with the one who is caught in sin through the process of repentance and restoration.

Now let's examine Paul's letter to the Colossians. Trying to figure out exactly what kind of theological error was causing so much trouble in Colossae is a messy, complicated task, but the heart of the problem was that their understanding of who Christ is and what he accomplished was woefully inadequate. As a result, Paul makes a stunning presentation of the fact that Jesus is God and that his death and resurrection was sufficient to save them completely.[78]

In Colossians 3, Paul builds upon what he has taught them about Christ and explains that the key to *kingdom obedience* is seeking the things of heaven from where Christ, our King, now rules. The old person, the one under the power of sin and death, has died, and now the true life of the believer is hidden with Christ in God (Col 3:3). Christ has interwoven their story with God's. So, they are to put on those deeds that reflect who they *are* in Christ, as they teach and warn one another with biblical wisdom and worship him through the singing of psalms, hymns, and spiritual songs (Col 3:16).

The lesson for the Colossians and for us is that every action throughout the day must be viewed as an opportunity to demonstrate the greatness of the redemption that Christ has provided for us and to show thankfulness to God for transferring us from the domain of darkness into the kingdom of his beloved Son—canceling the record of debt that was against us by nailing it to the cross.

We can conclude this investigation of *Kingdom Obedience* with the realization that Christ transforms us to demonstrates the greatness of the salvation that he provides. Because of this gift from our King, we must seek to live as his regents (agents) until he returns and completes the work he has begun in us. Sin and death are defeated enemies, and we must long for the day when Christ appears in glory, and they become non-existent enemies (1 Cor 15:42-58; Col 3:4).

Kingdom Mission

The ambassador's *kingdom mission* goes back to the creation mandate to extend God's reign throughout his creation. Christ brought us to new life, and the Spirit now emboldens us for the mission to proclaim the gospel of the Kingdom of God to all nations so that God will receive the worship he deserves from every tribe and tongue and people and nation (Rev 7:9-17). How then does *Kingdom Obedience* support the *Kingdom Mission*?

The primary goal of *Kingdom Obedience* is growing in holiness through which we will reflect the image of Christ in us (2 Cor 3:18-4:6). Growth in Christlikeness will lead to an ever-increasing satisfaction in God, but it also has missional motive. Paul explains in 2 Corinthian 3:18 that as we behold the glory of Jesus, we reflect more and more of his image, and as the glory of Jesus is reflected in our lives, the Spirit will use that reality as a confirmation of the truth that we proclaim to the lost about King Jesus (2 Cor 4:1-3).[79] Similarly, in Philippians 2:12-16, Paul exhorts the Philippians to demonstrate their salvation with fear and trembling because God is working in them so they will shine as lights in this sin-filled world.

In 1 Peter 2:9-10, Peter uses the language that Moses applies to Israel in Exodus 19 in order to encourage his readers that they are a prized possession of God and that they must proclaim his greatness even if persecution follows. Notice how he describes them: "But you are a chosen race, a royal priesthood, a holy nation, a people for his own possession, that you may proclaim the excellencies of him who called you out of darkness into his marvelous light." Because Christ has ransomed them in his sacrificial death and made them believers in God, they are now prepared to proclaim the greatness of what Christ has done as a kingdom of priests. Peter's instruction should lead us to conclude that God has transferred the kingly and priestly responsibilities of Jesus our King to the church. Jesus then empowers the church through his Spirit to extend his reign, by proclaiming his kingship[80] and by leading the nations to worship God.[81] This is our joyous task until he returns, and we reign with him as a kingdom and priests forever (Rev 5:9-10).[82]

God has promised to conform his people to the

image of his Son (Rom 8:28-30; Phil 1:6), so do not become discouraged when Bible confronts you with your sinfulness. Seeing our sin gives us the ability to see God's grace and come to embrace God's story as our story. In Christ, we have a new heart, a new behavior, and a new community through which the Spirit will strengthen us in the fight against sin and empower us to pursue holiness!

CONCLUSION

I hate Christian Laettner. I have a t-shirt to prove it. On March 28, 1992, he crushed my soul when he made the shot that has been unmercifully replayed by CBS in every March Madness montage since. I, however, have never watched it. When I see Grant Hill raise his arm to throw the ball, I drop my head and die a little inside.

I was a sophomore at the University of Kentucky at the time. I ate in the same cafeteria as the team, not that I really knew any of them. I can take you to the very spot in the Baptist Student Union where I saw that shot go in the basket. I will *never* forget.

You might be wondering, "What is wrong with this nut case? Hate seems like an extreme word? Why does it matter after all this time?"

Let me try to explain. That team was nicknamed "the Unforgettables" because the core of the team had endured one of the darkest times in Kentucky Basketball history, immortalized in the Sports Illustrated cover that read, "Kentucky Shame." On that night, we were on the biggest stage, and we were playing in the biggest game. We could go to the Final Four. We were no longer a "shame." I hope that you noticed the pronoun change. It was intentional. If you are from Kentucky or went to UK, every Wildcat basketball team is a part of who you are, but this team was special.

I have never scored a basket for the Wildcats and never will, but I use the first-person pronoun when talking about the team because Kentuckians like me gain a status, identity, and unity from the Wildcats that really nothing else in our state can give. So, when the family name was restored to prominence, the love grew deeper and more unrestrained. Folks like me did nothing to restore the family name. We did not work for it. We did not practice for it. We did not earn it. Yet, we benefitted from its restoration.

I believe that this neurotic example is a great analogy for the identity that Christians have as a result of the regenerating work of the Holy Spirit and their faith in Christ. We have an identity that we did not work for, practice for, or earn, but unlike the Wildcats, Christ *never* disappoints. He recreates us. He makes us truly human again. He empowers us to serve as his ambassadors. And, he guarantees us a place with him in his kingdom forever!

I guess in light of that great truth that I can just have a deep dislike toward Laettner and not hate. Nah. . . I still hate Laettner!

ARROW 5:
WHAT DOES THIS PASSAGE DEMAND OF ME?

"Wake up, the house is on fire!" No one in their right mind, after hearing this, would roll over and go back to sleep.

"I've got some bad news." The doctor's words can change everything in an instant.

"Will you marry me?" The question demands a response.

The authoritative words of Scripture carry even more weight. They demand a response. We must not approach the Bible like a stale, academic resource designed to bolster our knowledge about God for the sake of information alone. Rather, we should humbly allow the truths of Scripture to propel active obedience in a life of worship. This chapter is designed to discuss the way in which the Scriptures should bring about this response.

The four questions we have covered up to this

point have provided us a firm foundation from which to discover how we should respond:

- Arrow 1: *What does this passage say?*
- Arrow 2: *What did this passage mean to its original audience?*
- Arrow 3: *What does this passage tell us about God?*
- Arrow 4: *What does this passage tell us about man?*

We often jump into our Bibles and begin with the question Arrow 5 poses: "What does this passage demand of me?" Or usually, what does it "mean" to me? What am I supposed to do? How does this help me make decisions or cope with the pain of life? These questions are not bad; however, they are insufficient and the wrong place to *begin* the process of studying Scripture.

Consider what would happen if we read the following passages and started with Arrow 5's question:

Greet one another with a holy kiss. (Rom 16:16)

You shall surely put the inhabitants of that city to the sword, devoting it to destruction, all who are in it and its cattle, with the edge of the sword. (Deut 13:15)

When any one of you brings an offering to the Lord, you shall bring your offering of livestock from the herd or from the flock. (Lev 1:2)

One of two things would happen. Either you would make some bad (or embarrassing) decisions, or you would be downright confused. *I'm supposed to do what?*

The arrangement of the Arrows outlined in this book should reduce this confusion. They build on one another, so you would be foolish to take them out of order. First, summarize the main point of the passage (Arrow 1). Next, do the hard work of digging into the text and supplementary resources to determine what the text meant to its original audience (Arrow 2). Then, allow the main point of the passage clarify what the passage tells us about the nature and character of God and where it fits into God's grand story (Arrow 3). Finally, turn to fallen humanity in general and our own lives in particular to determine what the text tells us about ourselves and how our story intersects with God's story (Arrow 4).

Now, we are ready to apply the text to our lives. We know that "All Scripture is breathed out by God and profitable for teaching, for reproof, for correction, and for training in righteousness, that the man of God may be competent, equipped for every good work" (2 Tim 3:16–17). God brings profit from his word as we seek to hear and obey his voice.

Our goal in this book is to provide a practical tool to aid the average Christian, who has not had formal theological training, in discovering the word of God, feasting on its riches, and applying it to his or her life. For a reader to apply the Bible, readers in local churches must seek to apply it correctly, completely, and consistently. Let's consider each of these in turn.

APPLYING THE BIBLE CORRECTLY

In order to apply the Bible correctly, we must consider application as a direct result from the meaning of the passage we've considered. "If-then" statements are used to link two concepts in which the "then" statement is a logical response to the "if" statement. "If" one thing is true, "then" the second thing should be true as well. For example:

- *If* I forget to pay my bills on time, *then* I will get a late penalty;
- *If* my team wins the final game of the season, *then* we will go to the playoffs;
- *If* my kids have been disobedient during the day, *then* my wife is going to be tired and frustrated when I get home.

You get the point. The four Arrows we have considered up to this point pave the way to application by constructing an "if-then" statement for the reader.

Let's consider Psalm 51. David's prayer of repentance following his sinful relationship with Bathsheba and murder of her husband presents a clear "if-then" paradigm.

> Have mercy on me, O God, according to your
> steadfast love;
> according to your abundant mercy blot out my
> transgressions.
> Wash me thoroughly from my iniquity, and cleanse
> me from my sin!
> For I know my transgressions, and my sin is ever
> before me.
> Against you, you only, have I sinned and done what
> is evil in your sight,
> so that you may be justified in your words and
> blameless in your judgment.
> Behold, I was brought forth in iniquity, and in sin
> did my mother conceive me.
> Behold, you delight in truth in the inward being, and
> you teach me wisdom in the secret heart.
> (Ps 51:1–6)

You might use the Seven Arrows to analyze this passage in this way:

- Arrow 1: David acknowledges his sin before the Lord, fully admitting his sinful ways and begs God to cleanse him from sin.
- Arrow 2: The humble brokenness of Israel's greatest king in the face of his sin would teach the nation

of Israel about its desperate need for God's forgiveness.

- Arrow 3: God is powerful and faithful to forgive sin.
- Arrow 4: All people are sinful from birth and need the grace and mercy that can only come from God himself.

See, that was not hard! The truth of God's word is not meant to be a cryptic puzzle.

- If David acknowledges his sin and asks for forgiveness...
- If the nation of Israel remembers its need of cleansing...
- If God is willing and able to forgive sin...
- And if all people are in need of God's forgiveness...
- Then I should confess my sins to God and ask him to forgive me, knowing that he is faithful to forgive them completely.

As you notice, application is often found at the intersection of Arrows 3 and 4. God's character collides with our sinfulness and convicts us of areas in our life that need to change. Consider what happens when you are reading the book of Hosea. You might say in answer to Arrow 3, "God is faithful to love and redeem a people in spite of their sin." Your answer to Arrow 4 may be, "All people are unfaithful to God and pursue loves that never truly satisfy." How might you apply this passage?

Look at the intersection of these Arrows and you

might conclude something like this: "I am guilty of pursuing other loves instead of God, but he is relentless in his pursuit of me. He is far more glorious than all the lesser loves that I am pursuing, so I need to repent of my sin and worship him rightly."

Application is not always easy, however. Imagine that the Bible were a large mirror, reflecting back to the reader the proper response they should have to the passage. Consider three types of mirrors one might encounter when reading the Bible.

Clear

Clear passages have a straightforward, one-to-one correspondence to everyday life, and understanding the application will be easy (see Psalm 51, above). Notice that I did not say that they would be easy to *obey*. I said it would be easy to *understand what you should apply*! The work of God's Spirit is the only force capable of bringing a believer to the point of humility and brokenness required to submit to the authority of God's word. However, the application of the passage may be clear. Consider the following verses:

> *I therefore, a prisoner for the Lord, urge you*
> *to walk in a manner worthy of the calling to*
> *which you have been called, with all humility*

and gentleness, with patience, bearing
with one another in love. (Eph 4:1–2)

Rejoice always, pray without ceasing, give
thanks in all circumstances; for this is the will
of God in Christ Jesus for you. (1 Thess 5:16–18)

What do these verses demand of the reader? Well, just read the verse. It states quite clearly what God expects. If the reader works to define the terms used by the biblical authors, then the commands are obvious. Most often, passages like these occur in the wisdom books (such as Proverbs) or in the epistles (like Ephesians or Philippians).

Blurry

If the Bible were a mirror, some of the passages would be clear, but many would be blurry. These passages will likely not state explicitly what God demands from you. They will, much like the parables of Jesus, require taking the main theme of the text and converting it to a corresponding application. Blurry passages are typically found in narrative sections of the Bible (such as the Old Testament historical sections), the prophetic books, and many of Jesus' teachings. For example, consider the following passages:

After the death of Moses the servant of the LORD,
the LORD said to Joshua the son of Nun, Moses'
assistant, "Moses my servant is dead. Now therefore
arise, go over this Jordan, you and all this people,
into the land that I am giving to them, to the people
of Israel. Every place that the sole of your foot will
tread upon I have given to you, just as I promised to
Moses. From the wilderness and this Lebanon as far
as the great river, the river Euphrates, all the land of
the Hittites to the Great Sea toward the going down
of the sun shall be your territory. No man shall be
able to stand before you all the days of your life. Just
as I was with Moses, so I will be with you. I will not
leave you or forsake you. Be strong and courageous,
for you shall cause this people to inherit the land
that I swore to their fathers to give them. (Josh 1:1–6)

The kingdom of heaven is like treasure hidden in
a field, which a man found and covered up. Then
in his joy he goes and sells all that he has and
buys that field." Again, the kingdom of heaven is
like a merchant in search of fine pearls, who, on
finding one pearl of great value, went and sold
all that he had and bought it. (Matt 13:44–46)

What do these passages demand of the reader? The answer is a bit blurry. The Bible does not state explicitly what should be done. This challenge underscores why the *Seven Arrows* process is so important. Appropriate application can be made from these texts even though the Bible has not directly said what the reader must do. Consider the passage above from Matthew's Gospel:

- Arrow 1: The kingdom of heaven is such a great prize that a man will give up everything else to have it.
- Arrow 2: The hearers would have been stunned by the radical choices that these men would have made.
- Arrow 3: God, in his grace, offers his people a great treasure.
- Arrow 4: People who understand the riches of the kingdom of God are willing to give up everything to claim the prize.

Then...

- Arrow 5: I should thank God for the wonderful gift that is found by entering the kingdom of God and willingly give up anything that would keep me from treasuring the kingdom.

The reader is unlikely to face the choice to sell a field or buy a pearl, yet an appropriate application can be made to everyday life from this passage of Scripture. The same is true of the passage from Joshua. Sure, the reader is not taking a land and driving out inhabitants, but the passage clearly emphasizes the need to trust God to perfectly execute his plans and purposes—a lesson we all need to apply!

Broken

Some passages are so complex that the temptation is to discard them outright. They seem to be broken beyond repair. Frequently this results from the cultural distance between the modern reader and the biblical text. There are passages like this:

> If his offering is a goat, then he shall offer it before
> the LORD and lay his hand on its head and kill
> it in front of the tent of meeting, and the sons of
> Aaron shall throw its blood against the sides of the
> altar. Then he shall offer from it, as his offering
> for a food offering to the LORD, the fat covering
> the entrails and all the fat that is on the entrails
> and the two kidneys with the fat that is on them
> at the loins and the long lobe of the liver that he
> shall remove with the kidneys. And the priest shall
> burn them on the altar as a food offering with a
> pleasing aroma. All fat is the LORD's. (Lev 3:12-16)

> But I want you to understand that the head of every
> man is Christ, the head of a wife is her husband,

> *and the head of Christ is God. Every man who prays*
> *or prophesies with his head covered dishonors his*
> *head, but every wife who prays or prophesies with*
> *her head uncovered dishonors her head, since it is*
> *the same as if her head were shaven.* (1 Cor 11:3-5)

Space does not permit a detailed explanation of these passages nor is that the goal of this book; however, acknowledging passages like this exist in the Bible is important, and the reader needs to know what to do when encountering them. Here are some helpful pointers for how to handle hard passages:

Start simple

Begin with books of the Bible that are relatively clear rather than starting with books that are known to be challenging. For example, it would be wise to work through the Gospel of John before you start reading the book of Isaiah. Or, tackle the letter of Philippians before you take on Leviticus. Starting simple will help to build up confidence in using the *Seven Arrows* before working through more difficult books.

Think Big

Understand the grand story of God's work in the world. Chapter 3 provided a summary of the Bible's main story that tells how God is redeeming a people for himself through the death and resurrection of Jesus the Messiah. This macro-story will provide clarity on how the micro-stories fit together. For a more detailed summary of the central story of the Bible consult the first section of my (Matt's) book *Aspire: Developing and Deploying Disciples in the Church and for the Church.* It has a twelve-week workbook that will help explain God's work from creation to his ultimate return.

Use the Arrows

The process outlined in this book will help you dissect a difficult passage of Scripture. In fact, slowing down and using the Arrows is even more important when encountering difficult terrain. It's like a layup in basketball. When you are out on the court all alone playing against an imaginary defender, it's easy to get away with dribbling between your legs, wrapping the ball around your back, and floating a left-handed reverse layup off the backboard. Your coaches are not going to advise this, but it might just work in practice.

But, don't try that in a game, against real defenders, especially when the game is on the line! In that moment, slow down, execute the fundamentals, jump off the correct foot, bank it off the backboard, and watch it drop through the net.

You should do the same thing when reading the Bible. Clear passages (such as the ones mentioned above) may allow you to move quickly through the first four Arrows. Since they tell you exactly what is expected, you may easily get the point. It's not so with difficult passages. Slow down, read the text multiple times, work through the Arrows, consult external resources, and do the hard work required to make appropriate application.

Ask for help

Hard passages are hard for a reason. Some passages are unclear, and even scholars either don't understand them clearly or don't agree amongst themselves on the proper interpretation. Godly, Spirit-filled men and women disagree on the interpretation of a host of Bible passages. Even Peter said that Paul is hard to understand sometimes (2 Peter 3:14–16)! So, don't be discouraged if you come to a passage that does not make sense on your first reading. God has given us pastors and a church community for this reason. Go to them and ask questions about confusing passages.

APPLYING THE BIBLE COMPLETELY

Typically, when we think of application, we think of something to do. This mindset may limit the various ways God may call us to obey; however, application involves the entire person, not just a person's behavior. In fact, if we hyper-focus on behavioral changes only, we may miss the God-ordained ways that he chooses to bring about genuine transformation of his people's hearts and minds. This comprehensive application can be explained with the following terms: *Know, Be, Do.*

Know

The place to begin applying any passage of Scripture is in one's mind. Here we are not talking about the mere accumulation of abstract biblical facts but rather asking how the passage of Scripture shapes what we know to be true about God's character. After his masterful explanation of the gospel message, Paul shifts in Romans 12 to challenge the church in Rome to respond to God's grace by giving their lives to God as an act of worship. This process starts by being "transformed by the renewal of your mind" (Rom 12:2). Why would this be the place to begin? He begins with our minds because having a right understanding of the grace and mercy of God is sufficient motive for obedience. Without a right understanding of God, Paul knew that the church would not be able to bring about lasting change.

Arrow 3 helped us define what the text tells us about God. If this is true about God, *then* ask how God wants to use his word to change how you think about him. For example, in Luke 15 Jesus tells three "lost" stories which demonstrate his relentless pursuit of those that are wayward and rebellious—a lost sheep, a lost coin, and a lost son. Note from these passages that God's love prompts him to seek out those who have turned their backs on him (Arrow 3). You should also see yourself in the passage as you notice that humans are lost in a state of rebellion and sin and are in grave danger (Arrow 4).

A proper application of this text might look something like this: *I have always thought God was ashamed of me when I rebel and sin, so I tend to hide my sin from him. Through this passage, I need to remind myself that God loves me and pursues me in spite of my sin.*

Certainly, this knowledge should have real and lasting behavioral implications (for example, you should repent from your sins and fully embrace the love that God has demonstrated to you); however, change doesn't begin here. It begins in your mind as you see, understand, and stand in awe of the truth of the gospel of Jesus Christ.

Be

The head and the heart are connected. The great commandment establishes this relationship: "You shall love the Lord your God will all your heart and with all your soul and with all your mind" (Matt 22:37). This is not a linear progression, as if you first love God with your heart and then with your soul and then with your mind. Instead, the human makeup is such that the heart, soul, and mind are each an essential part of loving God, and they should be united in this pursuit.

The Bible speaks of the heart as being the core of a person—the seat of a person's emotions, thoughts, and the fuel for his actions. In the Old Testament, references to "the heart" refer both to the thoughts and the emotions. The context determines which of these two is being emphasized. Regardless of the emphasis, remember that behavior flows from the heart:

> For no good tree bears bad fruit, nor again does a bad tree bear good fruit, for each tree is known by its own fruit. For figs are not gathered from thorn bushes, nor are grapes picked from a bramble bush. The good person out of the good treasure of his heart produces good, and the evil person out of his evil treasure produces evil, for out of the abundance of the heart his mouth speaks. (Luke 6:43–45).

The writer of Proverbs, in a similar fashion, speaks of the heart as the "wellspring of life" (Prov 4:23). Everything flows from the heart.

This means that when we are seeking to apply a passage of Scripture, we should ask how God wants to use the passage to change our hearts. Here's what I mean. In Matthew, Jesus says,

> *Therefore I tell you, do not be anxious about your life, what you will eat or what you will drink, nor about your body, what you will put on. Is not life more than food, and the body more than clothing? Look at the birds of the air: they neither sow nor reap nor gather into barns, and yet your heavenly Father feeds them. Are you not of more value than they? And which of you by being anxious can add a single hour to his span of life? And why are you anxious about clothing? Consider the lilies of the field, how they grow: they neither toil nor spin, yet I tell you, even Solomon in all his glory was not arrayed like one of these. But if God so clothes the grass of the field, which today is alive and tomorrow is thrown into the oven, will he not much more clothe you, O you of little faith? Therefore do not be anxious, saying, "What shall we eat?" or "What shall we drink?" or "What shall we wear?" For the Gentiles seek after all these*

things, and your heavenly Father knows that you
need them all. But seek first the kingdom of God
and his righteousness, and all these things will be
added to you. "Therefore do not be anxious about
tomorrow, for tomorrow will be anxious for itself.
Sufficient for the day is its own trouble. (6:25–34)

It would be tempting to say immediately that the application of this passage is "Do not worry." While this statement is true, it is not enough. If you stop here, you can easily build a massive to-do list out of every biblical passage, inevitably crumbling under the weight of our incapability and shortcomings. A better application would look something like this:

- I should know that God provides for all things he has made, including me. (Knowledge-based application)
- I should trust God to meet my needs according to his great mercy and grace. (Heart-based application)
- I should not worry. (Do-application)

This process allows application of the principles from the text to be the shaping influences of behavior (the mind and the heart). We do this all the time in our daily lives. For example, I (Matt) know that I should wash the dishes at night so that my wife does not have to do it. But sometimes I just don't want to (shocking, I know!).

What fuel is powerful enough to get me off the couch and into the kitchen? First, I *know* that my wife loves me and sacrifices for our family and me and that my serving her provides a way to demonstrate the way that Jesus serves his people. Second, I *love* my wife. I treasure her and desire to find meaningful ways to demonstrate that love to her. My knowledge and my love compel me to do things that I might otherwise avoid or neglect. The same is true of the Bible—proper knowledge and heart change must lead to corresponding behavioral changes.

Do

Our actions matter. Knowledge of the truth and love for God are demonstrated in our behavior in the same way that the health of a tree is demonstrated by the quality of fruit that it produces. The order of Paul's letters helps us see this principle. For example, in the book of Romans Paul spends eleven chapters describing the glorious hope of the gospel and reminding the church of the grace given to it through the person and work of Jesus Christ. Then, in chapter twelve, he turns to exhorting the church on how they should respond to these truths.

> *I appeal to you therefore, brothers, by the*
> *mercies of God, to present your bodies as a*

living sacrifice, holy and acceptable to God,
which is your spiritual worship. (Rom 12:1)

The word "therefore" should alert you to the fact that Paul is building on what he has previously stated. What is the church to do? They are to offer their lives as living sacrifices. Chapters 12–16 in the book of Romans provide some clear action steps: serve the body, love one another, live in unity, pursue peace, submit to authorities, do not judge, make wise choices, and a host of other things.

Paul uses the same paradigm in the letter of Ephesians. He spends three chapters describing the sovereign grace of God in saving his people who were hopelessly and helplessly dead in trespasses and sins. Then, he writes

I therefore, a prisoner for the Lord, urge you
to walk in a manner worthy of the calling
to which you have been called (Eph 4:1)

Again, we notice the "therefore" which serves to connect what follows to the truths Paul has already established. Here, he says the result should be a life worthy of the calling Christians have received by virtue of God's grace. Chapters 4–6 define this "worthy life" by calling the church to unity, purity, honesty, forgiveness, love, submission, and perseverance.

Ask God to reveal what he wants you to do in light of the

things you read in the Bible. For example, Psalm 1:1–2 says,

Blessed is the man who walks not in the counsel of the wicked, nor stands in the way of sinners, nor sits in the seat of scoffers; but his delight is in the law of the LORD, and on his law he meditates day and night.

Clearly, God would desire for you to do something in light of this passage. You should *know* that God desires to reveal himself through his word, and your heart should *delight* in his word. But, don't stop there. If those things are true, then you should demonstrate them by spending time reading and applying the Scriptures to your life. Specifically, from this text, you should run to God's word for counsel and not to the "wicked," who are seeking to lead you astray. This *do*-based application should have real, discernable implications for how you spend your time.

APPLYING THE BIBLE CONSISTENTLY

Arrow 5, unlike some of the previous Arrows, is not a difficult question to answer. It will take far more time and effort to answer Arrows 1–4. If this work has been done well, the application of the passage should jump off the page and be abundantly clear on most occasions; however, moving the application from theory to practice will be difficult. We have all had the experience of knowing the things that we should do and simply not being able to do them consistently.

Be encouraged. You are on the right track. God has promised that his word will accomplish its good purposes in our lives (Isa 55:11). By faithfully committing to spend time with God in his word, we are tapping into the greatest tool the Spirit of God uses to bring about transformation in our life. Let's conclude this chapter by looking at two tools that God provides to aid us in faithfully applying the Scriptures to our lives.

Daily

In order to apply the Bible well, we must mediate on it deeply and consistently. Think of the last time you grilled out with friends. You can always tell the difference in a steak or piece of chicken that has had sauce poured on it while it was on the grill and the same piece of meat that has been marinating for the last 24-hours. The time spent marinating the meat results in a tasty treat.

In the same way, the word of God needs time to marinate in your mind and in your heart. For this to happen, you must do more than simply read a text early in the morning, answer the *Seven Arrows*, and then move on with the day. Instead, allow the text to bounce around in your mind throughout the day as you go about your daily routine.

One effective way to do this is to find ways to recall the passage throughout the day. Perhaps you could do this by writing it out on a note card and attaching it to the steering wheel of your car or placing it on your bathroom mirror. Another tool to aid in consistently reflecting on the word is memorization (I know that the word itself strikes fear in the hearts of many!); however, memorizing Scripture does not have to be intimidating. We all memorize things all the time (like song lyrics). This memorization allows the word to fill our minds and our hearts throughout the day. Pick a single verse or even a single phrase from a passage and commit to memorizing it over the course of a week. You will be surprised at how well you apply yourself to this task. You will also find encouragement from the way that memorization allows God's Spirit to bring the word to your mind at just the right time for you to apply it.

Community

A second aid to application is the church. God designed his church to be a context where his word resounds among his people. The value of the word is not merely seen in a Sunday sermon. In fact, the whole point of this book is to encourage you to feast on the word yourself. As a result, the word of God should provide the conversational vocabulary for the church. We should speak the word of

God to one another and encourage one another in our application of the word.

For example, you might read in the Scriptures one morning a reminder that God's love was demonstrated in his willingness to suffer and die for his enemies—those who hated him. As you reflected on this passage, you were convicted of your bitterness toward a family member that has wronged you and whom you have written off and haven't spoken to in years. You feel convicted that you need to pursue that person in love and apologize. Because you know apologies are painful and humbling, you start coming up with a host of reasons why you should not reach out to them. They have wronged you. If you call them, they will think they are getting away with it, and so on. So, because you long to obey God's word and know that, left to your own devices, you will probably not obey, you call a friend from church on your way to work. You recount your time in the word, the conviction that was brought about by God's Spirit, and ask them to check on you in a couple of days to ensure that you have followed up.

Or someone in your small group might share about his inability to make a hard life decision that involves taking a new job and moving his family. As you listen to the story, you recognize that he is hesitant because he is afraid of the perceptions of other people. He knows that this choice will disappoint his extended family, who will not see him as often, and his boss, whom he has grown to love. This person knows that God is calling him to take the new job, but he is paralyzed by fear. Rather than simply listening to the story and offering to pray for him, this setting provides a prime context for speaking the word into his life. You might say, "The writer of Proverbs tells us that 'the fear of man will prove a snare.' I think that you are ensnared by others' opinions and unwilling to be faithful to God as a result. Be reminded that God is to be feared above all else, even other well-meaning friends and family in your life." In so doing, the church is a conduit for the word to do its work among God's people.

You should never try to apply the Scriptures alone. To do so is to neglect one of the greatest forces to bring about genuine application—the church. Imagine what would happen if every local church was filled with people who were meaningfully reading God's word and seeking to help one another apply it to their lives each week. The Sunday gathering would pulsate with fresh life, beauty, and vitality.

CONCLUSION

I (Matt) remember my first few years following Jesus. It did not take long to figure out who the great men and women were. They were the ones with great gifts, or so I thought. The person who could preach a rousing sermon, the singer whose voice moved the congregation to tears, the leader who could mobilize people to tackle the next great challenge, or the pastor who had throngs of people hanging on his every word.

Much has changed in the last fifteen years. I've seen many people with great gifts disqualify themselves through heinous sin. I've seen people who seemed to have it all together fall apart. I've even seen myself run after being the next great leader, only to discover that it is not what it is cracked up to be.

Now, when I think of greatness, I think of faithfulness. I think of average men and women who have faithfully walked with Jesus for 40, 50, or 60 years. I think of those who love their God, their families, and their churches. Just being around people like this humbles me. They seem to have an aura of wisdom and godliness that I long to have. Life's chaos doesn't rattle them. They are steady, strong, and mature. I want to be like them when I grow up!

I've often thought about how to get there. How does a person go from where they are now to the level of maturity seen in faithful saints? The answer, I believe, is through daily submission to God's Spirit through his word. No one becomes mature overnight. No one obeys perfectly. But, what I can do is obey today. I can be faithful to do the one simple thing that God is calling me to do through his word today. We can all trust that God will be faithful to bring about transformation beyond all we can imagine if we are faithful to apply his word today.

ARROW 6:
HOW DOES THIS PASSAGE CHANGE THE WAY I RELATE TO PEOPLE?

This book was almost entitled *Six Arrows for Bible Reading*. The first four arrows were abundantly clear, as well as the question of application (Arrow 5) and the role of word of God in prompting prayer (Arrow 7). The more I (Matt) reflected on the Arrows, however, the more I saw the necessity of Arrow 6—*How does this passage change the way I relate to people?* Here's why.

The word of God should not be read or obeyed in isolation. Throughout salvation history, God has called a community to himself—not simply isolated individuals. The communal nature of the faith is seen most clearly in the New Testament church. The work of God is calling a people to himself through the finished work of Jesus not only unites us to God, our Father, but also to our fellow brothers and sisters in the church.

This connection is made most clearly in Ephesians 2. In

2:1–10 Paul establishes three main ideas. First, sin renders all mankind dead–hopeless and helpless unable to earn favor with God and rightly deserving of his wrath. Second, God sent Christ Jesus to pay the price for sin out of the sheer overflow of his grace and mercy. A person can be restored to God through faith in Christ. Third, those who repent of their sins by grace through faith are propelled to live a life of worshipful obedience that God has prepared in advance for them. We might refer to these as vertical truths because they tell us something that is true between God and mankind.

With this foundation in place, Paul shifts to a discussion of the horizontal implications of the work of Christ in Ephesians 2:11–22:

> But now in Christ Jesus you who once were far off have been brought near by the blood of Christ. For he himself is our peace, who has made us both one and has broken down in his flesh the dividing wall of hostility by abolishing the law of commandments expressed in ordinances, that he might create in himself one new man in place of the two, so making peace, and might reconcile us both to God in one body through the cross, thereby killing the hostility.

The result of sin is that mankind is separated from one another, living in tension, division, and strife. The result of the gospel is that all those who are in Christ can be united to one another by virtue of the fact that they have all been made a part of God's family. This fact demands that every passage of Scripture should be applied horizontally.

We created Arrow 6 to make this task explicit. This process is important in an age of individualistic Christianity. We can easily be led to believe that following Christ is something we do by ourselves:

- I trust Jesus to forgive my sins.
- I am granted eternal life when I die and will worship him forever.
- I am responsible for obeying God in this life.

While this is certainly true, we should also remind ourselves that:

- We, who are united to Christ, trust in him to forgive our sins.
- We, who are united to Christ, will spend eternity worshiping him together.
- We, who are united to Christ, have the joy of learning how to obey him together.

The corporate dimensions of faith and obedience to Christ are sadly neglected, leaving a wasted means of grace that God has provided to his people

There should be three built-in relationships in the life of every Christ follower that should shape and inform how we apply God's word: our families, our churches, and our relationships outside the church (our mission).

APPLYING THE BIBLE
TO OUR FAMILIES

When seeking to answer the question, *How does this passage change the way I relate to people?*, begin by considering the people closest to you. A spouse, children (if you have them), or your parents provide a natural set of relationships where we are forced to apply the reading of the Bible.

Those who are married are united in one flesh with another person. It cannot get any closer than that! As a result, there should no longer be any such thing as a personal sin, nor can there be any such thing as a private application of God's word. The word should have a spillover effect into the life of a spouse. The same is true for our children, who unfortunately often bear the brunt of sinful choices that are made by their parents. Children should hear the word in the home, and see the word have a transformative effect on their parents' lives.

Some passages make this easy. As a dad, if I read in Ephesians 6:4 that I should "not provoke my children to anger, but bring them up in the discipline and instruction of the Lord," then I know that this passage has direct implications for the way that I love and discipline my kids.

Other passages will require some intentionality in order to apply them to these vital relationships. When you read Philippians 2:3–4, you notice that you are called to "Do nothing from rivalry or conceit, but in humility count others more significant than yourselves. Let each of you look not only to his own interests, but also to the interests of others." While this text does not directly mention marriage and parenting, I would be foolish to not apply the text to those relationships. Where else is my selfishness, ambition, or conceit more often on display than in my home? For this reason, I would want to consider how God is exposing my sin and calling me to obediently serve my wife and my kids. As the text says, this will often mean laying aside my own interests so that I can serve them. A simple application might be—*I need to give up my lazy Saturday afternoon sitting on the couch and watching college football and take my kids out of the house on a hike so that I can give my wife a break at the end of a long week.*

What about those who are not yet married and do not have kids? If you are still at home living with your parents and under their authority, then this is a prime place to begin. If you are out your parents' home (for example, living in a college dorm room), then your roommate might provide the closest relational context for you to apply the Scriptures. Do not wait until you are married or have a family to begin to consider how your application of the word of God should affect those who are closest to you. For example, Colossians 3:23-24 says these words, "Whatever you do, work heartily, as for the Lord and not for men, knowing that from the Lord you will receive the inheritance as your reward. You are serving the Lord Christ." Again, this passage does not speak directly to relationships with parents or roommates, but consider the implications that it could have. Rather than shirking household responsibilities or doing them with a complaining spirit, the text may prompt you to do your work with excellence, with the understanding that you are pleasing God.

APPLYING THE BIBLE
TO OUR CHURCH

Next, we seek to apply the God's word to our church family. Remember that we said these relationships were expected for all Christians. Church is not an optional extra for God's people. Nor is it acceptable to argue that you are a part of the universal church but not a meaningful part of a local church body. Here's why.

Repeatedly, the Bible calls us to apply God's word in our relationships with one another. For example:

- *Accept one another, then, just as Christ accepted you (Rom 15:7).*
- *Teach and admonish one another will all wisdom (Col 3:16).*
- *Carry each other's burdens (Gal 6:2).*
- *Be patient, bearing with one another in love (Eph 4:2).*

- *Encourage each other (1 Thess 4:18).*
- *Be devoted to one another in brotherly love (Rom 12:10).*

The list could go on and on. These are some of the simplest passages in the Bible to *understand* how to apply. They are some of the most difficult, however, to *actually* apply. They require you to do the hard work required to apply them to real life people in the context of actual relationships.

This is why the local church matters. You cannot apply these commands in isolation. I can't be patient with someone that I have never met, nor can I be devoted to another person when I "attend" church by watching a sermon on TV while sitting on my couch. I can only apply these commands when I am in a real, committed relationship with Mark, or Joe, or Christina.

Not only that, but I can really only apply Scriptures like these when I am in a relationship with people over an extended period of time. I can't forgive someone else until I have been in relationship with him long enough for him to sin against me. Then, we can do the hard work of working through conflict and rebuilding a broken relationship in a way that models the gospel of Jesus Christ. This is why the consumeristic nature of much of the church today hinders the work of applying the Scriptures. If you change churches at the slightest conflict, move to a new job every two years, and simply build relationships with people exactly like you, then you will never fully learn the beauty of obedience to God's word.

Now, it is certainly true that you are not likely to be able to know and apply every passage of Scripture with every person in your local church family. But you can certainly apply it to someone—perhaps your small group, your Sunday School class, or some friends that live in your neighborhood. Consider the following story Jesus tells in Mark 12:41-44:

> And he sat down opposite the treasury and
> watched the people putting money into the
> offering box. Many rich people put in large
> sums. And a poor widow came and put in two
> small copper coins, which make a penny. And
> he called his disciples to him and said to them,
> "Truly, I say to you, this poor widow has put in
> more than all those who are contributing to the
> offering box. For they all contributed out of their
> abundance, but she out of her poverty has put
> in everything she had, all she had to live on.

It's hard to apply this passage in isolation, right? How do you give without someone to give to? The church provides a glorious context for the application of this passage. Like the widow, we should give out of our poverty to support the needs of our brothers and sisters. Whether we are blessed with abundant material possessions or are unsure of where our next meal will come from, we are all able to give. In the church, we see real people in need of our care and generosity. You could rightly apply this text by looking at the needs of others in your local church family and asking God to prompt you to someone in need of your generosity.

Or, I might read the story of Job and notice the foolish counsel provided by Job's friends in the face of his suffering. While we may not know someone suffering to the same extent as Job, every church is filled with people burdened by the weight of their own form of suffering. We would appropriately apply the book of Job to remember to speak a word of encouragement to a member of our church, reminding them that God is sovereign and in control and that he has not abandoned them.

All it takes is a bit of intentionality, and the opportunities for applying God's word to his church will become endless. We could add another dimension to our chart to reflect the need to apply the Bible to our church relationships.

APPLYING THE BIBLE
TO OUR MISSION

Finally, we are all given a God-ordained mission. We do not only apply the Scriptures for our own benefit and the benefit of the church, but also for the sake of those who do not yet know and worship Jesus. God places his Spirit within his people and sends them into the world to declare and demonstrate the good news of Jesus Christ. The word of God must work its way out of our lives through missionary obedience, or else we will grow spiritually complacent and prideful. For example, it is easier to think that you are a forgiving person when you spend your time around people that are much like you. If you live on mission, you will soon find yourself in relationship with people who are far from God and who will consistently wrong you or take advantage of you. It is in the context of these difficult relationships that your forgiveness will be tested. The more you care for people the more you will be convicted of sin and called to greater levels of holiness.

People who are far from God come in all shapes and sizes. Ideally, you are already in relationship with them. If not, consider this your first exercise in practicing Arrow 6. We read in 1 Peter 2:9-10:

> But you are a chosen race, a royal priesthood, a holy nation, a people for his own possession, that you may proclaim the excellencies of him who called you out of darkness into his marvelous light. Once you were not a people, but now you are God's people; once you had not received mercy, but now you have received mercy.

You are chosen by God to declare the beauty of God to people far from God. To not live a life of mission is to be disobedient to God. This is not something superstar Christians do, rather it is the expected outcome of the life of all of God's people.

When you start to apply this text, you are likely to find at least four different types of people in need of seeing and hearing the gospel:

- *The Religious*–People who think that they have a relationship with God based on their ability to keep rules and avoid the typical sins associated with those far from God (for example, many church-goers who live in the religious south).
- *The Worldly*–People who are comfortable and content with a life apart from God and who see no need for the message of the gospel (for example, many business professionals or college students).
- *The Marginalized*–People who are broken, wounded, discarded, or neglected due to poor choices they have made, their ethnicity, lifestyle, or the consequences of living in a sin-soaked world (for example, single-moms, former convicts, the homosexual community, or certain ethnicities).
- *The Antagonistic*–People who have rejected the gospel (or some pseudo-version of it), find its truth claims offensive, and are hostile to any attempt at their conversion (for example, former

church-goers who have abandoned the faith, family members who doubt the genuineness of your conversion, or adherents to other religions).

It is important for us to consider how we might apply the word of God to these people. Relationships are vitally important. Without the context of a genuine and loving relationship, any attempt to articulate the gospel is going to seem manipulative and self-seeking. Even when there is a genuine relationship, it is still likely that suffering and persecution will result. This must not mean that we do not try, however. Let's consider how we might apply the Bible to each of these types of people.

The Religious

The problem with religious people is that they are going to think they have heard it all before. The good news is that they are going to be open to hearing about the Bible and are not likely to reject you outright. In this context, genuine self-disclosure is likely to be the best means of discussing the Bible with them. It might go something like this:

I was reading a really familiar passage this morning from Proverbs. "Trust in the LORD with all your heart, and do not lean on your own understanding.

> *In all your ways acknowledge him, and he will make*
> *straight your paths" (Prov 3:5-6). I know you have*
> *read that passage a hundred times and so have I,*
> *but this morning I was freshly convicted of how*
> *often I trust my own plans and purposes rather*
> *than depending on God to lead me. I am praying*
> *that God would help me trust him more today.*

This approach exemplifies great relational wisdom. If you were to say, "I've noticed that you seem to depend on yourself a lot around work. As a Christian, you should trust God more," you might get punched (And probably should be!). By humbly confessing your own need for growth, you allow the Spirit to bring conviction and life change in the other person.

The Worldly

Those who do not have a felt need for the gospel are unlikely to respond to the approach above. Sure, they might smile and nod, but it's more to appease you than anything else. The big question for worldly individuals is "Why?" Why follow Jesus and obey the Bible when life seems fine without him? They are going to need to see you consistently apply the Bible to your life and articulate why you make the choices that you do. For example,

> *I know that the common practice is for business*
> *professionals in our line of work to travel and*
> *spend the night in hotels 3 or 4 nights a week. I*
> *just can't do that. Time with my wife and family*
> *is far too important for me to be away from home*
> *that often. Also, business travel and nights in*
> *hotel provide far too many opportunities for me to*
> *compromise my integrity and harm my marriage.*
> *God's word tells me that if my eye causes me to*
> *sin, then I am to cut it out. So I'm not willing to*
> *climb the corporate ladder if that is the cost.*

In this short conversation, you have applied the word of God effectively to the life of someone who wants nothing to do with God. You have shown both *how*, and more importantly, *why* you have chosen to obey. You are not likely to see fruit in the first conversation, but over time and with consistency you may. Often it will require an experience of suffering to cause the person to see their need for the message you have been sharing. For example, as soon as your co-worker, who has chosen to climb the corporate ladder, finds that his marriage is falling apart, he will likely remember the contrast he sees in your life.

The Marginalized

The challenge in talking about God's word with the marginalized is that they are likely to feel like you are talking down to them, regardless of whether you intend to be or not. This is to be expected—many of them have borne the brunt of scorn and hostility from supposed Christians in the past. This means that the most important thing you can do when applying the Bible in your mission to the marginalized is to exemplify wisdom. Thankfully, this should be easy for those who are truly submitting to the word. The word of God will be a tool by which God consistently humbles you, and this humility can have a spillover effect in the lives of others. Consider Luke 18:9-14:

> He also told this parable to some who trusted in
> themselves that they were righteous, and treated
> others with contempt: "Two men went up into
> the temple to pray, one a Pharisee and the other
> a tax collector. The Pharisee, standing by himself,
> prayed thus: 'God, I thank you that I am not like
> other men, extortioners, unjust, adulterers, or
> even like this tax collector. I fast twice a week; I
> give tithes of all that I get.' But the tax collector,
> standing far off, would not even lift up his eyes
> to heaven, but beat his breast, saying, 'God, be

> merciful to me, a sinner!' I tell you, this man went
> down to his house justified, rather than the other.
> For everyone who exalts himself will be humbled,
> but the one who humbles himself will be exalted."

This text presents a ready-made opportunity for you to apply the word to the marginalized. You might say something like this in response to a single-mom who lives next door who has made the comment that you and your family always seem to "have it all together:"

> I was thinking about that when I was reading my
> Bible this morning. Jesus was telling a story about
> two men who went to pray: one was a religious
> leader and the other was a notorious sinner. The
> religious guy prayed, thanking God that he was not
> like the other sinner. The known sinner was praying,
> begging God to show him mercy since he knew that
> he was in need of God's grace. You might look at
> me and think I am the religious leader in the story,
> but actually I see myself as the known sinner. You
> see, I need God to help me remember that I am no
> better than anyone else and that I need God's mercy
> as much as anyone. You see the thing is, I KNOW
> that my family and I don't have it all together,
> but rather, we have Jesus holding us together.

You have just leveled the playing field, putting yourself on the same plane as the single-mom who lives next door. She may have looked at your family and thought that you "had it all together." She may have assumed that you subtly thought you were better than she is. She almost certainly thinks that most in the church judge her for her choices. Over time, conversations like this will likely win you the right to talk more openly about the gospel.

The Antagonistic

By definition, these people do not want to hear about the word of God and are likely to react with anger if you try to convert them. This situation presents a real challenge when trying to apply the word of God to their lives. What should you do? Certainly you don't try to pick a fight by being abrasive. You should try to earn the right to be heard by living a compelling life. Your life can (and should) prompt questions from those far from God. Peter makes it clear how we are to respond in 1 Peter 3:14-17:

> But even if you should suffer for righteousness'
> sake, you will be blessed. Have no fear of them,
> nor be troubled, but in your hearts honor Christ
> the Lord as holy, always being prepared to make
> a defense to anyone who asks you for a reason for

> *the hope that is in you; yet do it with gentleness*
> *and respect, having a good conscience, so that,*
> *when you are slandered, those who revile your*
> *good behavior in Christ may be put to shame.*
> *For it is better to suffer for doing good, if that*
> *should be God's will, than for doing evil.*

We should live a distinctive life that causes others to ask questions. These questions are primary catalysts for conversations about the gospel with those who are antagonistic to the faith. They may hate the message, but they can't discount your life. It might go something like this:

> *You were asking the other day about why I had*
> *downsized cars and was not driving that new*
> *truck anymore. Well, the short answer is we can't*
> *afford it. We made the decision last month that*
> *my wife was going to stop working so that she has*
> *more time to devote to raising our children and*
> *volunteering at a crisis pregnancy center. Giving*
> *up her income was a hard choice for us. I know*
> *you hate when I talk to you about God, but that is*
> *the answer to your question. We believe that God*
> *calls us to store up treasures in heaven and not*
> *on earth, so we are going to make costly sacrifices*
> *now and trust that God knows what is best for us.*

There is little guarantee that this will "work." You may still be laughed at. You may be mocked. Your co-worker may walk away. But any of those options is better than being silent. You have been faithful to declare the word to him, and you can now trust God with the results.

As you consider each of these areas also remember that the Bible is not something you only apply through the spoken word. Of course it is that, but it is also more. You apply the Bible through your words *and* through your actions. So do not merely consider how you can speak the truth of the passage you are seeking to obey but also how you can model it through a distinctive life. This might include things like:

- Going the extra mile at your job to show your co-worker that you do all things as an act of worship to God;
- Serving your spouse when they have sinned against you to show them that you want to model a Christ-like love in your home;
- Volunteering at a neighborhood after-school program to show that the love of Christ extends to the least of these.

CONCLUSION

You may be tempted to think that this chapter is out of place in a book designed to help people study the Bible. We are convinced that this is the reason that so much of what parades as Bible study is nothing more than Bible trivia or a form of self-help. We often read the Bible and expect it to do little more than fix our problems. But this is not what the Bible is for. God is not concerned with simply fixing our problems. He is concerned about seeing us transformed by the work of his Spirit so that we worship him rightly and give our lives to see others do the same. *Mission fuels Bible reading.* It drives you to the word and keeps you in the word.

Recently, I had the privilege of visiting one of the mission sending agencies for the Southern Baptist Convention. Throughout the building, there were pictures on the wall. Not just random pictures that you would buy in a store—they were all of people (often individual people) framed and hanging on the walls. As we walked with our tour group, many from the group pointed to people on the wall and said, "Hey, I know that guy!" or "I recognize that girl!" At the end of the tour, the guide told us that the pictures were intentional. He said, "We did not want people to think of us as simply another agency where money is sent. When people think of us, we want them to think of people. Real people. People are not likely to invest in a nameless and faceless mission, but they will give passionately to people they know and love."

The same is true for Bible study. It is vital that these types of people take on a specific name and face for you, or else you are not likely to apply the word of God to that relationship. As long as mission stays theoretical, it will never be accomplished. When reading the Bible think, *I wonder how I can apply this passage to my co-worker Joe or to my neighbor Anna?* Such missional obedience necessitates the seventh, and final arrow, which asks "How does the passage prompt me to pray?"

ARROW 7:
WHAT DOES THIS PASSAGE PROMPT ME TO PRAY?

Our world is filled with ways for people to talk to us—from phone calls, to text messages, to social media posts. These messages may fill you with joy and happiness or with fear and worry.

Hey babe, I love you and hope you have a great day.

Mom and Dad are praying for you this week as you start back to school.

Let's plan to go to the pool today around 3pm.

Each of these messages prompts us to answer. It's hard to imagine getting a message from someone you love and not wanting to reply back.

The Bible declares the word of the King of the universe, God himself, to you and me. This message is far from trite. His word is living and active, speaking to us in a personal way. What a glorious privilege to consider that God would humble himself by speaking in words that people like us can understand! We have been given grace every time we meet

God in his word, hear what he is saying, and apply that word so that our lives increasingly reflect the image of Christ.

The purpose of this final chapter is to consider how we should reply to God's word. The answer is simple— you respond back to him in the same way that you would respond to a message from a loved one. You talk to him.

Arrow 7 asks you to consider, *What does this passage prompt me to pray*? However, you should not merely conclude your time in Bible reading with prayer. This is also where you should start. The process of seeing the Bible clearly and applying it consistently is a gift of God's grace, empowered by his Spirit. So we must seek God in prayer and ask Him to help us read well.

The Seven Arrows guides you to have a plan for your prayers as you conclude your time in the word as well. Rather than clamoring the dark to know what to say or simply repeating the same thing that you said yesterday, you can pray biblically informed prayers derived from your response to God's word.

Praying the Bible back to God may seem like a strange undertaking. *I mean, doesn't He already know what He wrote? Why does he need me to say it back to him?* There are a number of reasons why praying the Scriptures is a necessary and fruitful way to build a healthy prayer life. Consider the following benefits that praying the Scriptures provide: *awareness of God's conviction, consistency, confidence, specificity, diversity, reinforcement,* and *simplicity.*

CONVICTION

It is easy to get in a rut with your prayer life. You are often prone to pray about the things that are at the forefront of your mind. While this is not necessarily wrong, it can subtly cause you to miss other things that the Spirit wants to show you. God's sovereignty will be seen in your choice of Bible reading. You will be surprised at the way that God will orchestrate your reading so that you read a passage that will bring to mind something you needed to hear but perhaps would have failed to think about on your own. The word of God is "living and active" and is therefore capable of illuminating areas of your life that you would not otherwise see. Therefore, the Bible will be used to confront your sinfulness, bring conviction, and prompt you to pray with a humble heart, trusting that God is willing and able to forgive.

CONSISTENCY

Maybe you struggle to maintain consistency in your prayer life like I do. You may find that you grow passive in your prayer life and only pray when you think about it. So many things clamor for our attention each day. We have family responsibilities, work assignments, TVs, computers, and text messages which each clamor for our attention on a regular basis. If we are not careful, we simply don't think about prayer often. A steady diet of the word of God will provide a consistent reminder about your need for prayer. Connecting prayer and Bible reading allows you to build momentum in your spiritual disciplines and ensure that you are consistently engaging in these vital practices the Lord has given us to conform us to his image.

CONFIDENCE

Praying the Scriptures also provides assurance that you are praying in line with God's good purposes. Jesus tells us that if we ask anything in his name, he will do it (John 14:14). This is not simply some magical mantra meaning you can tag "in Jesus name" on the end of anything you pray and trust that God will answer it. Instead, God will do anything you ask that is in line with God's purposes and plans. As a result, we should desire to pray in such a way that our words align with God's purposes.

How do you know that you are doing this? The best path to praying in line with God's will is to trust the words of Scripture. He has provided them as a clear guide into his character, thoughts, and plans for the world. We can trust that when we pray in line with the Scriptures, we are praying in line with God's purposes. This should infuse your prayers with great confidence.

For example, following a job loss you may be tempted to pray, *God, I pray that you would give me a new job soon.* This is a valid prayer, but it may not be God's plan in this situation. A better idea, however, would be to pray the Scriptures. You may say, *God, you tell me in your word to not be anxious about my life, what I will eat or what I will drink, not about my body, what I will put on (Matt 6:25). I pray that you would help this job loss to teach me to trust you more, knowing that you will always provide for my needs.* You can have great confidence that this prayer is in line with the good purposes of God because he has clearly told you these things in the Scriptures.

SPECIFICITY

Our prayers are often generic and vague. We may find that we are praying the same phrases over and over again such as "forgive me of my sins" or "thank you for my family" or "bless my day." There is nothing necessarily wrong with these prayers but they lack specificity. Asking God to forgive you for your anger and bitterness towards your spouse is far more specific than asking God to forgive you of your sins in general. The Scriptures will provide a tool for revealing specific needs for your prayers and will help you tell God exactly what you feel and think.

DIVERSITY

Sometimes our prayers can grow stale and routine. We pray when something bad happens, such as a friend being diagnosed with cancer, a co-worker getting hurt in an accident, or a wayward teenager rebelling. These needs certainly necessitate prayer, but there is so much more to a robust, biblical prayer life. Your mind often lacks clarity, and so whatever is the primary focus of your attention is the thing you are often tempted to pray for while neglecting other matters that are equally important but which are not at the front of your mind at any given moment. For example, you may be more prone to pray for your child's first day of school than you are to pray for their future spouse. We should also be consistent in our prayers of thankfulness to God, our affirmations of his character and worth, our acknowledgment of our sinfulness and need for the gospel, and our fervent hope in his mission to see the lost saved. These types of prayers will often be the fruit of a prayer life based on the Scriptures.

REINFORCEMENT

Praying the Scriptures also reinforces the passage you are reading. You are more likely to recall a passage if you talk to God specifically about it. This also provides a way of heightening the importance of the things you have read. Prayer forces you to do more than recite theological facts. You must personalize the passage and ask God to transform your heart so that you can obey its meaning. Healthy prayers will be a means of aiding you in memorizing a biblical passage, as well.

SIMPLICITY

Finally, praying the Scriptures requires thought and intentionality. Perhaps this is uncommon for you and you typically pray about whatever is on your mind at any given moment. Arrow 7 should force you to slow down, think about your prayers, and construct meaningful prayers to God. There are two ways that you can intentionally pray the Scriptures that you have read.

Through Repetition

You may choose to pray the exact words of Scripture back to God. For example, you may pray Psalm 118:28-29:

> God, "You are my God, and I will give thanks
> to you; you are my God; I will extol you.
> Oh give thanks to the LORD, for he is good;
> for his steadfast love endures forever."

Often, you can simply change a pronoun in the passage in order to personalize it. In the passage from Hebrews below I have taken out the plural pronouns found in the original text and constructed a prayer with personalized pronouns (noted in bold):

> God I pray "since **I am** surrounded by so great
> a cloud of witnesses, let **me** also lay aside every
> weight, and sin which clings so closely, and let
> **me** run with endurance the race that is set before
> **me,** looking to Jesus, the founder and perfecter of
> **my** faith, who for the joy that was set before him
> endured the cross, despising the shame, and is seated
> at the right hand of the throne of God" (Heb 12:1-2).

Some passages lend themselves to become prayers more readily than others. The Psalms are easily constructed as prayers since they were originally composed as songs to God. Passages that have a clear statement about God's character also provide a useful method for praying prayers of thankfulness. You can pray Exodus 34:6–7 by saying:

> God you are "merciful and gracious, slow to
> anger, and abounding in steadfast love and
> faithfulness, keeping steadfast love for thousands,
> forgiving iniquity and transgression and sin."

Finally, passages that contain a clear exhortation are ready-made for prayer:

> God help me to think on "whatever is true, whatever
> is honorable, whatever is just, whatever is pure,
> whatever is lovely, whatever is commendable, if
> there is any excellence, if there is anything worthy
> of praise," help me to think on these things (Phil 4:8).

Through Composition

You can turn other passages into prayers by using the Arrows outlined in this book. You can simply say the truths discerned in Bible study back to God. For example, consider Colossians 3:1-2:

If then you have been raised with Christ, seek the
things that are above, where Christ is, seated at
the right hand of God. Set your minds on things
that are above, not on things that are on earth.

A prayer shaped by this passage might sound something like this:

God, I acknowledge that Christ is no longer dead
but has been raised by your mighty power and
is enthroned in the heavens. By virtue of my
faith in Christ, I too have crucified my sinful self
and have been raised to a holy life" (Arrow 1).

Paul reminded the church in Colossae that they
were to set their minds on the things of God
and not on the things of this life (Arrow 2).

I know that you are holy and pure and desire
your people to reflect your glory (Arrow 3).

But, life in this broken world makes it
hard for me to focus on you (Arrow 4).

I pray that you would, by the power of your
Spirit, transform my mind so that I love
the things that you love and think about

the things that bring you joy (Arrow 5).

I also pray that you would use me to show others that the things of God are of far greater worth than the things of this world (Arrow 6).

Thank you for what you are showing me in your word. Amen.

This progression provides a robust foundation for developing your prayer life. Start by praying something that is true (Arrows 1 and 2). Then, move to adoration of God's character and worth (Arrow 3). From there, acknowledge your own brokenness and neediness, particularly as it relates to the passage you have just read (Arrow 4). Ask God to change your heart so that you can obey the command found in the passage (Arrow 5). Conclude with a missional prayer—asking God to use you to communicate his glory to others (Arrow 6).

It may be wise to walk through this process, even for passages that are already worded as prayers. It will help you memorize the Arrows and pray well-rounded prayers that do more than simply ask God for things. The prayers also declare things to be true, affirm the worth of God, admit your need for his grace, and shape your heart for missionary living.

Journaling is not something that comes naturally to

me (Matt). I have at least a dozen journals that I have written on less than 10-pages. I start strong but can never maintain the consistency I desire.

The *Seven Arrows* provide a built-in journaling guide. Simply write the date and the passage in a journal and then doodle the *Seven Arrow* images below. Beside each Arrow, write out thoughts and ideas from God's word. This journaling process will provide a lasting legacy of God's work in your life. As you journal over the years, you will be able to find encouragement from God's work in your life, see reminders of thoughts you had at earlier points in your life, and have a tool to note the ways that God is changing you and conforming you to the image of Christ.

PUTTING IT ALL TOGETHER

We set out to write a book that would serve the church in reading the Bible well. It is designed to be practical and leave you with a plan for sitting down with your Bible, reading through any book, understanding what you've read, and being able to apply it to your life. *Seven Arrows* provides an organized plan for reading effectively. Now, as we conclude, we want to try to put it all together. Think of this as being able to eavesdrop on our quiet time as we journal using the *Seven Arrows* to study the Bible. We will provide you an example from five different types of

Scripture so you can see how we would use the Arrows in different genres.

Old Testament Narrative

Begin by reading Deuteronomy 8:1–10. Here's how I might use the Seven Arrows to guide me through this passage.

What does this passage say?

God humbled his people on the way to the Promised Land in order to teach them to trust him to fulfill his promises.

What does this passage mean to its original audience?

The nation of Israel would have been reminded that, in spite of the trials and pain of the wilderness wandering, God was going to be faithful to give them the Land and had been faithful in teaching them to trust him along the way.

What does this passage tell us about God?

God is faithful to his people in spite of their sin and doubt.

What does this passage tell us about man?

People are prone to doubt God's provision and often need times of trial and pain to teach them to depend on God.

What does this passage demand of me?

I should trust God to be faithful to his promises to me and use whatever season of life I am facing to develop deep faith in God

How does this passage change the way I relate to people?

When facing any trying circumstance, I should boldly speak of my firm confidence in the Lord and the ways that he is transforming me through adversity

What does this text prompt me to pray?

God, I thank you for your faithfulness to your people. As I saw today, you kept your promises to the nation of Israel. You were kind enough to lead them on a long journey through the wilderness to teach them to trust in you. I praise you for keeping true to your word, even though I am so prone to being hypocritical with mine. I pray that you would continue to do whatever necessary to teach me to depend on you, and that I would speak openly of your work in my life when I am around those who are far from you. Amen

Wisdom Literature

Now read Proverbs 10:19–21. At first glance, these proverbs might seem clear but they can often be more confusing than you might think. Here are the Seven Arrows applied to this passage.

What does this passage say?

The way people choose to use their words demonstrates what is in their hearts and can often have consequences for others.

What does this passage mean to its original audience?

The people of God would have heard much the same thing as a modern reader. They would have understood that their words mattered and would have been reminded of the need to speak wisely.

What does this passage tell us about God?

God speaks words of wisdom to his people.

What does this passage tell us about man?

People are likely to sin with their words and hurt others by speaking foolishly.

What does this passage demand of me?

I should choose my words carefully knowing that they can have painful and lasting consequences. Not only that, but my words provide evidence for what is in my heart, so I should repent of the heart motives that drive my foolish speech.

How does this passage change the way I relate to people?

I likely need to repent to people whom I have wounded with my words. Additionally, I should consider how my words can "feed many" with blessing and encouragement.

What does this text prompt me to pray?

God, today I read a very practical passage of Scripture that reminded me of the way that my words could cause harm to others. I know that you always speak wisely and you have been gracious to me today to speak and convict me of my sin. I am often foolish in the words I choose and this causes harm to others. I think about the way that I misrepresented myself in the conversation with my neighbor yesterday as I bent the truth to try to make myself look better than I actually am. I pray that you would continue to remind me of the power of my words and convict me quickly when I wound others. Amen.

Prophecy

Prophecy is one of the most challenging genres in the Bible. Consider Ezekiel 36:16-21. Let's apply the Seven Arrows to this passage.

What does this passage say?

The nation of Israel defiled God's name and reputation in the Promised Land; therefore, God gave them over to judgment, and they were exiled among the nations.

What does this passage mean to its original audience?

It is almost impossible to imagine the devastation that the people of God would have felt as a result of the Exile. Their sin had caused God to send the nations to judge them. Now their identity and prized land had been taken from them, and they were a shamed and humiliated minority scattered among the nations.

What does this passage tell us about God?

God will act in judgment to protect his reputation because his name is holy.

What does this passage tell us about man?

Even when lavished with the grace of God, people are prone to turn from God and act in such a way that profanes his holy name.

What does this passage demand of me?

I am equally guilty of receiving the grace of God and the gift of his Spirit and living in such a way that dishonors his name. The judgment that was due my sin was poured out on Christ, and this grace should motivate me to bring glory to his name.

How does this passage change the way I relate to people?

In every relationship, God's name is on the line. People often form perceptions of God's character based on my life. I need to take that into account as I interact with my neighbors, coworkers, and even random strangers.

What does this text prompt me to pray?

God, you have reminded me today that you are holy. This holiness required you to judge the nation of Israel for their willing disobedience to you in the Promised Land. I know that you acted out of your love for your people because you wanted them to understand the consequences of their actions. And, you wanted the other nations to know that you are God and that your name was not to be profaned. I know that I profane your name often in calling myself a Christian and living in willing idolatry. I thank you that Christ absorbed the judgment that I deserve. I pray that this truth would not make me passive, however. I pray that it would motivate me to live a life of holiness each and every day. I pray that others would be drawn to you because of the transformation they see in my life. Amen.

Parables

Now let's turn our attention to one of Jesus' favorite teaching methods—a parable. Read Luke 14:25-33.

What does this passage say?

Anyone who wants to be a disciple of Jesus should first consider the cost of following him, which includes renouncing everything one has to follow him.

What does this passage mean to its original audience?

These two illustrations (building a tower and fighting a battle) would have been far more common in Jesus' day than in ours. Our day may have different illustrations, but the point remains unchanged. Before you do anything, you must make sure that you understand the cost of the decision and that you are prepared to pay that price.

What does this passage tell us about God?

God calls people to leave everything and follow him, as an act of his grace and to do so is a wise choice.

What does this passage tell us about man?

People are prone to say that they desire to follow Jesus without fully understanding the total claim that he then has on their lives. As a result, they are often quick to turn back when they see how radical the path of discipleship truly is.

What does this passage demand of me?

I must consider what I am unwilling to lay aside in order to follow Christ completely.

How does this passage change the way I relate to people?

When I invite people to follow Jesus, I must remind them that this decision is going to radically reshape every facet of their lives.

What does this text prompt me to pray?

God, you have been gracious in calling me into relationship with you. I know that you are a great God and following you is so much better than anything else my heart treasures. My sin causes me to foolishly cheapen your commands and settle for a mediocre level of discipleship that is not fit for you. I pray that you would give me the grace necessary to lay aside my idolatrous business aspirations that drive me to minimize my commitment to you and sacrifice my integrity. I pray that the choices I make would demonstrate to others that you are so much greater than anything the world has to offer. Amen.

Letters

Finally, let's read a section from one of Paul's letters found in Colossians 1:15–20.

What does this passage say?

All things were created by Jesus, through Jesus, and for Jesus; therefore, Jesus deserves to be preeminent in all things.

What does this passage mean to its original audience?

The Colossian church would have been reminded that though they and Paul were suffering for their faith in Jesus, this suffering was worthwhile due to the supreme glory of Jesus.

What does this passage tell us about God?

There is nothing in all of creation more glorious than Jesus Christ.

What does this passage tell us about man?

People need to be reminded of the preeminence of Christ because we often make other things more valuable than him.

What does this passage demand of me?

I should be humbled by the awe-inspiring splendor of the person of Jesus Christ. Meditating on his glory should cause my heart to esteem him as preeminent above all things in my life.

How does this passage change the way I relate to people?

This passage shows me that Jesus is the only way of reconciling man to God. This should cause my life to be engulfed with a passion to declare the worth of Christ to all people so that all may know Him.

What does this text prompt me to pray?

God, it pleased you to reconcile fallen men and women to yourself through the work of your son, who is the exact imprint of your nature. Your glory is seen in the fact that you created all things, sustain all things, and allow all things to give you glory. I pray that you would be preeminent in my life. Remove those things that clamor for my attention and distract me from giving you the glory that you deserve. Allow my life to reflect your glory to a watching world. Amen.

Our sincere hope is that after seeing the use of the Arrows to walk through these five passages, you think, *I can do that! That really doesn't seem that hard after all.* We promise to not take offense, and that it will not hurt your pastor's feelings if you say, "Now, I know how you've been doing that all this time. Today, when I heard your sermon, I actually knew how you did it. It didn't seem like a magic trick anymore. Now, I know how you did that!"

CONCLUSION

Cliffs Notes on books were once a slacker's best friend. Why waste your time reading the actual book when the abbreviated summary can be provided for you? We often approach Bible study in this fashion. We allow other people to summarize the Bible for us, provide some cursory anecdotes, and then tell us how we should apply the passage in question to our lives.

The task of this book has been altogether different. Rather than summarizing a passage of Scripture for you, providing commentary on that passage for you, and then challenging you to obey what it says, we have attempted to teach you how to do the summarizing and commentating for yourself and not just the obeying! We have sought to apply the familiar proverb, "Give a man a fish, and you feed him for a day; teach a man to fish, and you feed him for a lifetime." We would propose a similar proverb, "Give a man a deer, and you feed him for a while; teach a man to hunt (aim his arrows properly), and you feed him for a lifetime." In other words, "Preach a man a sermon, and you feed him for a day; teach a man to study the Bible for himself, and you feed him for a lifetime!" Our hope is that *Seven Arrows* provides you with the "hunting tools" that will help you aim your Bible study arrows to hit the target of properly interpreting the Scriptures for the rest of your life. The fruit of this book should have immediate implications for a number of key areas in your life.

YOUR PERSONAL
TIME WITH GOD

Clearly, your time with God has been the main focus of this book. Our hope is that you feel confident to sit down with your Bible (and a good cup of coffee!) and mine treasures from the Scriptures each and every day. However, no one can make this happen for you. The best plan is pointless if you do not actually make time to sit down and meet with God each day. Most people find it helpful to have a predictable time set aside for this practice. We all know that if we do not have a plan that the busyness of life will often crowd out any meaningful time with God.

This is why it may be advisable to begin the day with some time alone with God. Start by getting up a few minutes early, avoiding checking any email or messages, and carving out 15-30 minutes to read the Bible and journal through the *Seven Arrows*. This practice will allow you to have a Godward focus at the beginning of each day and will provide a text of Scripture for you to mediate upon as you go. You may also want to set aside a separate time at the end of the day to read back over the same passage. It may bring to mind things you have meditated on throughout the day.

If you are new to reading the Bible, you may wonder where to begin. This is a wonderful question. You may choose to approach the Bible like any other book and simply start at the beginning, in Genesis. This approach will allow you to move sequentially through God's redemptive plan as seen through the pages of Scripture. However, this approach is not without its challenges. Some of the most difficult terrain in all of the Scriptures lies is the first third of the Bible—particularly once you enter the books of Leviticus and Numbers. It is likely that you will grow weary of the consistent repetition and also confused by the vast cultural differences between yourself and the nation of Israel. Unfortunately, this difficulty causes many passionate Bible readers to give up quickly.

The books of the New Testament are probably going to be more familiar for the average Bible reader. The fact that Jesus' life and work provides the key to understanding all of the Bible means that you may find one of the Gospels a better place to start. These books (Matthew, Mark, Luke, and John) each tell the story of Jesus from his birth to his resurrection. The books are not identical, however. They each tell the story from a different perspective by highlighting different facets of Jesus' ministry. You can begin in any of the four. Typically, it is best to use *Seven Arrows* on smaller segments of the Scripture. Rather than reading one chapter at a time, you could read an individual story. Most English Bibles will help with this task by breaking up the chapters into thematic units under a major heading. For example,

- Matthew 14:1-12 "The Death of John the Baptist"
- Matthew 14:13-21 "Jesus Feeds the Five Thousand"
- Matthew 14:22-33 "Jesus Walks on the Water"
- Matthew 14:34-36 "Jesus Heals the Sick at Gennesaret"

These divisions provide a good guide to dividing up the Scripture passage.

Smaller New Testament letters also provide a place to begin utilizing *Seven Arrows*. Letters such as Ephesians, Philippians, or Colossians are succinct, clear, and loaded with significance for the modern reader. You can pick any of these letters and read them from major heading to major heading and work through them in two or three weeks of consistent Bible reading.

One word of caution is necessary. For you to reap the benefits of *Seven Arrows*, it is always best to read through books of the Bible in their entirety. As you saw in our discussion of Arrows 1 and 2, the passages of Scripture are not written like a dictionary. You do not simply look up a topic of interest and find a verse that addresses that situation. Instead, you should attempt to read through an entire book of the Bible before moving on to another book. This plan will allow you to see the main points the author is making, recognize the way that he develops an argument, and see how he connects the various themes of the book to one another. This does not mean that you have to work through all 66 books in order, but it does mean that you should not read Mark 6, followed by Exodus 32, and then skip to Ephesians 6. This random method of Bible reading will often leave you confused and frustrated.

YOUR DISCIPLESHIP OF OTHERS

We pray that this book will not simply be a tool that you use in your personal time with the Lord. We are hoping that this book creates a domino effect in your life so that you will begin to help others learn to read and understand the Bible for themselves. You can, and should, expect that others might feel as insecure about their efforts at Bible reading as you might feel at times. Many young believers desire to read and understand the Bible, but they need help.

You are now prepared to offer that help. Certainly, we hope that you will recommend picking up this book and that it serves to aid in reading the Bible. But, we are actually hoping for much more. They are likely going to need some help in this process—someone to hold them accountable for reading, to answer questions that they might have along the way, and to encourage them as their lives begin to transform as a fruit of their time in God's word.

One of the best ways to accomplish this goal is to find someone who will practice the *Seven Arrows* with you. All this takes is agreeing upon a book that you will read together. By together, we do not mean that you should actually read together in the same room. Instead, agree upon a section of Scripture, and read it over the course of a given week. Then, pick a time to meet together to discuss what you have read. For example, you could begin reading the book of Ephesians together. There are approximately seven major headings in chapters 1-3, which would provide a week's worth of daily devotional reading. You might ask a friend to read this over the course of the coming week and then pick a time to meet to discuss the thoughts from your journal through the *Seven Arrows*. This process would provide encouragement, accountability, and direction as you each seek to grow in Bible reading.

YOUR TIME LISTENING TO BIBLICAL TEACHING

A third area of your life where you should see growth as a result of using the *Seven Arrows* is in your time listening to sermons or other forms of Bible teaching. We have sought to free you from an over-dependence on sermons and Bible teaching and to show you that you can do much of that work on your own. This goal, however, is not intended to devalue sermons. In fact, daily and consistent Bible intake should make you a better listener during sermons and Bible studies. Our prayer is that you would act like the Bereans, who in Acts 17 diligently searched the Scriptures after hearing Paul and Silas teach in order to confirm the things they had heard.

If you know the passage your pastor will be preaching from each Sunday, then you can work through the text using *Seven Arrows* prior to hearing the sermon. This practice will allow you to come to the sermon with a soft heart that has already been broken by the message of the passage in question. It can also be a useful tool in confirming your study throughout the week. Imagine your joy if you were able to listen to a sermon and think, *Yeah. That's exactly what I thought this week!* Typically, your pastor will still be able to provide depth and clarity to the text that you may not have seen, but if you work through the text effectively, you will have done much of the work prior to the sermon and will be encouraged by the fruit of your study.

Before long, you may find that you are more confident in teaching the Bible to others as well. Often, people think that a seminary degree is required in order to lead a Bible study or small group at their local church. This is not the case. A person who studies the Bible daily using *Seven Arrows* will quickly find that he is capable of teaching others through books of the Bible. Do not be surprised if God uses this process to call you into higher levels of leadership in your local church than you currently hold.

YOUR LIFE ON MISSION

Finally, we are praying that *Seven Arrows* will propel you to a life on mission. We have sought to infuse this process with a missionary passion in such a way that it would be quite clear to you that you should not simply study the Bible for yourself. You should seek to grow in understanding and applying the Bible so that you can be used by God to declare and demonstrate the gospel message faithfully everywhere you go.

This witness should begin in the circles of influence closest to you—your family and close friends, your co-workers or schoolmates, or anyone else that you see on a regular basis. Allow the final three Arrows to prompt you to demonstrate a life that is in the process of being transformed by the word of God. Ask God to fill you with a passion to declare his word to those that you see daily. Perhaps, you might even use *Seven Arrows* to guide a family devotion each morning as you seek to train your children to know and love God's word.

The spillover effect should extend far beyond your closest friends and family. A genuine commitment to being transformed by God's word will raise your spiritual antenna and make you more aware of the work of God around you everywhere you go. This may include a random conversation with a stranger in a store checkout line or an extended conversation with a mom while your kids play on the playground. You will be amazed at the host of ways that God will use his word to inform these conversations and give you words to say at just the right time. Not only that, but you will grow increasingly comfortable with communicating the gospel to others due to your familiarity with God's word. This will allow you to speak words of grace and truth to those who are far from Christ.

YOU CAN DO THAT

Reading God's word is not a magic trick. It is the God-ordained process by which his Spirit conforms his people to increasingly reflect his image. It is not the sole terrain of pastors, seminary students, and theologians. It is the ground we all must travel. You can do it. It will certainly require intentionality and work, but you must not lose heart. Read the compelling promise of the prophet Isaiah concerning the word of God:

For as the rain and the snow come down from
heaven and do not return there but water the
earth, making it bring forth and sprout, giving
seed to the sower and bread to the eater, so shall
my word be that goes out from my mouth; it shall
not return to me empty, but it shall accomplish
that which I purpose, and shall succeed in
the thing for which I sent it (Isa 55:10-11).

God's word will accomplish his purpose in his people. We pray that *Seven Arrows* will be a tool to assist you in seeing that great promise fulfilled in your life.

ABOUT THE AUTHORS

Matt Rogers lives in Greenville, South Carolina with his wife, Sarah, and their four children where he serves as one of the elders of The Church at Cherrydale (www. tccherrydale.com). His teaching and writing ministry is birthed out of his passion to equip the church to mature as worshipers of God. Matt completed his undergraduate education at Furman University (BA in Psychology) and graduate studies at Gordon-Conwell Theological Seminary (MA in Counseling) and Southeastern Baptist Theological Seminary (MDiv in Pastoral Ministry). He completed a PhD at Southeastern with an emphasis in North American Missions and Church Planting in 2015. Matt speaks throughout North America and is the author of a number of books including *Aspire: Transformed by the Gospel.* Learn more about matt at http://mattrogers.bio.

Donny Mathis

Donny Mathis lives in Taylors, South Carolina with his wife, Amber, their son, Trace, and their daughter Hallie. He is a Professor of Christian Studies at North Greenville University (www.ngu.edu) in Tigerville, South Carolina, where he has taught for twelve years, and is also a lay elder at The Church at Cherrydale (www.tccherrydale. com). Donny is a graduate of the University of Kentucky (BS in Mechanical Engineering) and The Southern Baptist Theological Seminary (MDiv in Higher Education and PhD in New Testament, Language, Literature, and Theology). Donny wrote his doctoral dissertation on *Abraham and the Exile in Galatians* 3:1-14. Follow Donny on Twitter @ dmathisii.

ENDNOTES

Introduction

1   Kevin DeYoung, *Taking God at His Word: Why the Bible is Knowable, Necessary, and Enough, and What that Means for You and Me* (Wheaton: Crossway, 2014), 121.

2   See D.A. Carson, *The Gagging of God: Christianity Confronts Pluralism* (Grand Rapids, MI: Zondervan, 1996); Jonathan Leeman, *Reverberation: How God's Word Brings Light, Freedom, and Action to His People* (Chicago: Moody, 2011).

Arrow 1

3   Just in case you were wondering, here is a list that groups the books of the Old Testament according to their dominant style. Law: Genesis–Deuteronomy (clearly these books also have a large amount of historical narrative as well); Historical Narrative:

Joshua–Esther (these books will include other styles like proverbs, poetry, and speeches but are dominated by stories); Songs and Proverbs: Job–Song of Solomon (Songs) and Lamentations; Prophecy: Isaiah–Malachi (Take note that prophecy is not primarily about predicting the future but about preaching a message to Israel about her disobedience and God's faithfulness.) Here is a list for the New Testament. Historical Narrative: Matthew–Acts (these books will include other styles like proverbs, poetry, and speeches but are dominated by stories); Letters: Romans–Jude; Prophecy: Revelation.

4   Robert H. Stein, A Basic Guide to Interpreting the Bible: Playing by the Rules, 2nd ed. (Grand Rapids: Baker, 2011), 68–74. Stein provides a more complete description of the types of language that are used in the Bible. That discussion is also the basis for the discussion above.

5   See J. Scott Duvall and J. Daniel Hays, Grasping God's Word: A Hands-On Approach to Reading, Interpreting, and Applying the Bible, 3rd ed. (Grand Rapids: Zondervan, 2012), 54–61, 71–81; Stein, 87–98, 199–205. The items in this list come from these two outstanding resources.

6   A clause is a group of words that has a subject and a verb (predicate). If that group of words has a subject, a verb, and expresses a complete thought, it can be classified as an independent clause (sentence). If that group of words

is introduced by a subordinating conjunction (a term we will describe below), it will be classified as a subordinate (or dependent) clause because it does not express a complete idea and, therefore, cannot stand alone as a sentence. If this definition is confusing, I think that the examples below will provide helpful clarification.

7   This illustration is a modification of one that I received from Dr. Robert Stein.

8   In chapters 1–4, I have translated the New Testament passages from Greek to English myself.

Arrow 2

9   Readers of the Bible often question which version they should use for their personal Bible study. There is not a single correct answer to this question. We would advise readers to utilize the *Seven Arrows* while reading a version of the Bible that strives to reproduce the language of the original authors while doing so in a style that is clear to modern readers such as: English Standard Version, New American Standard Bible (1995), New International Version, or the Holman Christian Standard Bible.

10 These categories come from the explanation of the cross-references in the ESV Heirloom Reference Edition from Crossway Publishers. If your Bible has

cross-references, it will have some type of explanation, like this one from my Bible, for the system that the editors are using.

11 The Exile, in a sense, begins with the destruction of the Northern Kingdom of Israel in 722 BC by the Assyrians and continues with the destruction of the Southern Kingdom in 586/587 BC by the Babylonians. The prophets, however, state clearly that God is the one who is sending them into exile and is the one who will restore them with a deliverance like the Exodus.

12 Carl G. Rasmussen, *Zondervan Atlas of the Bible*, rev. ed. (Grand Rapids: Zondervan, 2010), 13.

13 Chad Brand, et. al., ed., "Denarius," *Holman Illustrated Bible Dictionary* (Nashville: Holman Bible, 2003), 412.

14 Larry Walker, "Festivals," *Holman Illustrated Bible Dictionary*, 569–72.

15 Wikipedia can be a great resource in many areas, but it should not be trusted as a source for your Bible study because anyone can make edits to the entry even if their information on the topic is incorrect. The likelihood of finding accurate information is much higher in the other materials that I referenced.

16 This Bible dictionary preceded the *Holman Illustrated Bible Dictionary* cited above and was written before the conservative shift in the Southern Baptist Convention was complete. This volume can still be quite helpful as long as you realize that not every article was written

by people who believe in the inerrancy of Scripture.

17 These references are not endorsements of the websites as a whole but are acknowledgments about the availability of resources.

18 Gary Burge, *John*, The NIV Application Commentary (Grand Rapids: Zondervan, 2000), 226–27.

19 Ibid., 255–56.

20 Gerald Borchert, *John 1–11*, New American Commentary, vol 25A (Nashville: Broadman and Holman, 1996), 291; Burge, 227.

21 Borchert, 291; Burge, 228–29.

22 Borchert, 295–96.

23 Ibid., 296. See Borchert's conclusion: "Jesus' claims are reminiscent of the praise songs to God in the Psalter, where the Lord is epitomized as the Light of life (Ps 56:13), where light is symbolized as God's victory over the traumas of life (Pss 37:6; 44:3), and where darkness is described as no problem for God (Ps 139:12; cf. Isa 4:7). In addition, light is patently related to the concepts of salvation in the Bible (e.g., Ps 27:1; Isa 58:8; cf. John 1:5; Acts 26:18; 2 Cor 4:4-6; Eph 5:14; 1 John 1:7)" (296).

Arrow 3

24 John Piper, *Don't Waste Your Life*, Group Study Edition (Wheaton, IL: Crossway, 2010), 99-106.

25 Although many have written about the grand narrative of the Bible and many others have influenced my (Donny's) thinking on these matters, particularly the writings of N. T. Wright. See especially N. T. Wright, *The New Testament and the People of God*, Christian Origins and the Question of God, vol. 1 (Minneapolis: Fortress, 1992). I would also like to thank friends and colleagues, like Brian Henderson; Curt Horn; Bill Murray; Jeff Rankin; Ben Skaug; and, obviously, Matt Rogers for their help in sharpening my thoughts on these matters through conversations that have taken place over the course of many years. I thank God for you all.

26 See 1 Kings 11:6; 15:26, 34; 16:7, 18-20, 25–26, 29-34; 21:25–26; 22:51–53; 2 Kings 3:1–3; 8:16–19, 25–27; 13:2–9, 10–13; 14:23–27; 15:8–9, 17–18, 23–24, 27–28; 16:1–4; 17:2; 21:1–16, 20; 23:32, 37; 24:9, 24:19

27 1 Kings 15:9–16; 22:41–44; 2 Kings 12:1–3; 14:1–6; 15:1–5; 32–35; 18:1–12; 22:1–2.

28 D. A. Carson, *The Gospel of John*, Pillar New Testament Commentary (Grand Rapids: Eerdmans, 1991), 115: "God's word in the Old Testament is his powerful self-expression in creation, revelation, and salvation, and the personification of that 'Word' makes it suitable for John to apply it as a title to God's ultimate self-disclosure, the person of his own Son."

29 Ibid., 126–27: "The 'tent of meeting' was the place where the LORD 'would speak to Moses face to face

as a man speaks with his friend' (Exod 33:11). In Exodus Moses hears the divine name spoken by God himself, and this is followed by God's word written on two stone tablets. Now, John tells us, God's Word, his Self-expression has become flesh."

30 Ibid., 131–34; Borchert, 123–24.

31 Stein, 147–49.

32 For a more detailed description of these ideas see, Christopher J. H. Wright, *Knowing Jesus through the Old Testament* (Downers Grove, IL: IVP Academic, 1995), 55–64.

33 N. T. Wright, *Simply Jesus: A New Vision of Who He Was, What He Did, and Why He Matters* (New York: Harper One, 2011), 170–71.

34 Ibid., 170.

35 Ibid., 170–71.

36 Ibid., 171.

37 Wright, *Knowing Jesus*, 181–91.

38 Ibid., 183–84.

39 Ibid., 184–85.

40 Ibid., 185–87.

41 Ibid., 187–91. N. T. Wright, *Jesus and the Victory of God*, Christian Origins and the Question of God, vol. 2 (Minneapolis: Fortress, 1996), 491–92.

42 Wright, *Jesus and the Victory of God*, 491–92.

43 Ibid.

44 Wright, *Simply Jesus*, 127–29; 163–65.

45 See Wright, *Victory*, 560–62.

46 The words italicized in this paragraph are intended to highlight the attributes of God that we have emphasized in this section.

47 Gen 12:1–3; Isa 27:6, 60:1–22; Gal 3:13–14, 23–39, 6:11.

48 John B. Polhill, *Acts*, New American Commentary, vol. 26 (Nashville: Broadman, 1992), 63.

49 Ibid., 64; Robert H. Stein, *Luke*, New American Commentary , vol. 24 (Nashville: Broadman, 1992), 39–40, 45–46. See Acts 4:1–31; 6:8–8:4; 9:10–19; 16:19–40; 21:37–22:21; 26:30–32; 28:23–31.

50 Polhill, 64–65.

51 Isa 44:3; Ezek 36:22-32; 37:1-14; 39:35-39; Joel 2:28-32.

52 Grant Osborne, *Revelation*, Baker Exegetical Commentary on the New Testament (Grand Rapids: Baker Academic, 2002), 33–34.

53 Ibid., 32.

54 Ibid., 32–33.

55 Ibid., 34–35.

56 Ibid., 31–34, 46–49.

57 Ibid., 48–49.

58 Ibid., 49.

Arrow 4

59 Scot McKnight, *The King Jesus Gospel: The Original Good News Revisited* (Grand Rapids: Zondervan, 2011), 34-36, 137-38.

60 For a detailed description of these issues, see Wayne Grudem, *Systematic Theology: An Introduction to Biblical Doctrine* (Leicester, England: IVP; Grand Rapids: Zondervan, 1994), 439–53; Millard J. Erickson, *Introducing Christian Doctrine*, L. Arnold Hustad, ed. (Grand Rapids: Baker, 1992), 155-70.

61 Erickson, 157.

62 Grudem, 440–41; Piper, 23–42.

63 Grudem, 442.

64 Ibid., 443.

65 Erickson, 167; Grudem, 449–50: "Every single human being, no matter how much the image of God is marred by sin, or illness, or weakness, or age, or any other disability, still has the *status* of being in God's image and therefore must be treated with the dignity and respect that is due to God's image-bearer" (Ibid, 450; emphasis original).

66 Grudem, 443.

67 McKnight, 138.

68 Ibid.

69 Daniel I. Block, *Deuteronomy*, NIV Application Commentary (Grand Rapids: Zondervan, 2012), 182–84.

70 Grudem, 494–96; Erickson, 201–03.

71 Grudem, 496–97.

72 Ibid., 497.

73 Erickson, 180.

74 Grudem, 445.

75 Piper, 99–105.

76 McKnight, 138.

77 Joshua Harris, *Why Church Matters* (Colorado Springs: Multnomah, 2004), 20–35. Harris' exposition and reflection on Ephesians 5 and its implications for the church has significantly influenced my thinking in this section.

78 John B. Polhill, *Paul and His Letters* (Nashville: Broadman & Holman, 1999), 338.

79 McKnight, 140-41.

80 Remember how we discussed in Arrow 3 that the church conquered the world through the preaching the gospel of the Kingdom of God.

81 McKnight., 138; Mike Cosper, *Rhythms of Grace: How the Church's Worship Tells the Gospel Story* (Wheaton, IL: Crossway, 2013), 50-51.

82 McKnight., 141.

61260681R00165